Honoria and Mammon by James Shirley

As it was represented by young Gentlemen of quality at a private entertainment of some Persons of Honour.

James Shirley was born in London in September 1596.

His education was through a collection of England's finest establishments: Merchant Taylors' School, London, St John's College, Oxford, and St Catharine's College, Cambridge, where he took his B.A. degree in approximately 1618.

He first published in 1618, a poem entitled Echo, or the Unfortunate Lovers.

As with many artists of this period full details of his life and career are not recorded. Sources say that after graduating he became "a minister of God's word in or near St Albans." A conversion to the Catholic faith enabled him to become master of St Albans School from 1623–25.

He wrote his first play, Love Tricks, or the School of Complement, which was licensed on February 10th, 1625. From the given date it would seem he wrote this whilst at St Albans but, after its production, he moved to London and to live in Gray's Inn.

For the next two decades, he would write prolifically and with great quality, across a spectrum of thirty plays; through tragedies and comedies to tragicomedies as well as several books of poetry. Unfortunately, his talents were left to wither when Parliament passed the Puritan edict in 1642, forbidding all stage plays and closing the theatres.

Most of his early plays were performed by Queen Henrietta's Men, the acting company for which Shirley was engaged as house dramatist.

Shirley's sympathies lay with the King in battles with Parliament and he received marks of special favor from the Queen.

He made a bitter attack on William Prynne, who had attacked the stage in Histriomastix, and, when in 1634 a special masque was presented at Whitehall by the gentlemen of the Inns of Court as a practical reply to Prynne, Shirley wrote the text—The Triumph of Peace.

Shirley spent the years 1636 to 1640 in Ireland, under the patronage of the Earl of Kildare. Several of his plays were produced by his friend John Ogilby in Dublin in the first ever constructed Irish theatre; The Werburgh Street Theatre. During his years in Dublin he wrote The Doubtful Heir, The Royal Master, The Constant Maid, and St. Patrick for Ireland.

In his absence from London, Queen Henrietta's Men sold off a dozen of his plays to the stationers, who naturally, enough published them. When Shirley returned to London in 1640, he finished with the Queen Henrietta's company and his final plays in London were acted by the King's Men.

On the outbreak of the English Civil War Shirley served with the Earl of Newcastle. However when the King's fortunes began to decline he returned to London. There his friend Thomas Stanley gave him help and thereafter Shirley supported himself in the main by teaching and publishing some educational works under the Commonwealth. In addition to these he published during the period of dramatic eclipse four small volumes of poems and plays, in 1646, 1653, 1655, and 1659.

It is said that he was "a drudge" for John Ogilby in his translations of Homer's Iliad and the Odyssey, and survived into the reign of Charles II, but, though some of his comedies were revived, his days as a playwright were over.

His death, at age seventy, along with that of his wife, in 1666, is described as one of fright and exposure due to the Great Fire of London which had raged through parts of London from September 2nd to the 5th.

He was buried at St Giles in the Fields on October 29th, 1666.

Index of Contents

To the Candid Reader
Dramatis Personae
Scene – Metropolis or New-Troy
HONORIA AND MAMMON
ACT I
SCENE I – A Street
SCENE II – A Room in Honoria's House
ACT II
SCENE I – A Room in Aurleia Mammon's House
SCENE II – A Room in Honoria's house
ACT III
SCENE I – A Room in Traverse's House
SCENE II – A Room in Aurelia Mammon's House
SCENE III – A Room in Traverse's House
SCENE IV – Another Room in the Same
SCENE V – A Room in Honoria's House
ACT IV
SCENE I – The Street Before Traverse's House
SCENE II – The Country – Maslin's House
SCENE III – The Same – Traverse's House
ACT V
SCENE I – Metropolis – A Guard Room
SCENE II - A Prison
JAMES SHIRLEY – A CONCISE BIBLIOGRAPHY

TO THE CANDID READER

A Small part of this Subject, many years since had drop'd from my pen: But looking at some opportunities upon the Argument, I thought some things more considerable might be deduced; and applying my self further, at times of recess, I felt it grow and multiply under my imagination: Nor left I it then (the matter being so pregnant in it self) till I form'd it into such limbs and proportions as you now see it. Modesty after this, invited me to cover it, and to cut off many impertinences, and purge some humour, that saye, I confess, unhandsomely upon it.

What is now presented, I hope will appear a genuine and unforc'd Moral, which though drest in Drammatique Ornament, may not displease, in the reading, persons of ingenuity, such whose nature is not to create prejudice, where they intend a recreation. And in the confidence of that, I do not repent the superstructures I have made, my pains, nor expences that have attended to bring it to this. It is now publique to satisfie the importunity of friends, I will onely adde, it is like to be the last, for in my resolve, nothing of this nature shall after this, engage either my pen or invention.

The reason why I make no particular Dedication to any Friend, is, because I aim my general respect to all, whose favours and civilities have oblig'd me. At this none will be offended, where none hath the precedence: And to conclude with the most serious truth, I know not any, that love me so little, whom the payment of my so mean addresses would satisfie, as to clear me upon the account of his friendship. Let this suffice at present from him, that is

Your Servant,
JAMES SHIRLEY

DRAMATIS PERSONAE
Conquest a Colonel,   }
Alworth a Scholar,   } Lovers of Lady Honoria
Alamode a Courtier,   }
Fulbank a Citizen,   } Suitors to Lady Mammon.
Maslin a Countreyman,   }
Travers a Lawyer, servant to Mammon and Honoria
Squanderbag.
Phantasm, Gentleman-usher to Lady Mammon.
Aurelia Mammon
Dash the Lawyers Clark
A Captain.
A Serjeant.
Soldiers.
Countrymen.
Honoria.
Mammon.

SCENE – Metropolis or New-Troy

ACT I

SCENE I – A Street

Enter **ALWORTH** and **PHANTASM**.

ALWORTH
Tis not far off, 'Ile aske this Gentleman.
Can you instruct me, sir, where the great
Lady Aurelia Mammon lives?

PHANTASM
Yes sir, I can.

ALWORTH
Pray do me the civility.

PHANTASM
Have you
Affaires with her, my friend in black.

ALWORTH
Have you
Relation to the Lady, Sir?

PHANTASM
She ownes me
A Gentleman-usher, with your pardon Sir,
Are not you inclining to a Scholar?

ALWORTH
I have spent time i'th Academy.

PHANTASM
The Academy?
Another beggar,
I did think so by your serious face, your habit
Had almost cosened me, and your hair, they are
Of the more Court edition, this is
A beggar of the upper forme of Learning,
Your business with my Lady,

ALWORTH
If you please

To prepare my access—

PHANTASM
'Tis to no purpose,
My Lady keeps no Library, no food
For booke-worms, I can assure you that,
Learning is dangerous in our Family,
She wo'not keep a Secretary for fear
Of the infection.

ALWORTH
Does she keep no foole?

PHANTASM
Yes, yes, and knaves;

ALWORTH
I thought so,
In which classe is your name, I beseech you?

PHANTASM
We enjoy equal priviledges, indeed the knave
Makes somewhat more on's office, but my Lady
Is not so nice, so we can bring Certificates
That we are sound, and free from the infection
Of book's, or can lay down our understandings,
And part with that unnecessary stuffing
I'th head, (you know my meaning) or renounce
The impious use of humane art and knowledge,
We are in a capacity of imployment;
Perhaps you may, on these terms be admitted
With your Philosophy, and things about you,
To keep her horse, de'e observe?

ALWORTH
A faire preferment!

PHANTASM
The fittest here for men of art, or if
You can keep counsell and negotiate handsomely
The amorous affair of flesh and blood;
(There you may exercise your parts of Rhetorique.)
How lies your learning that way? 'tis an office
Many grave persons have submitted to,
And found it a smooth path to court preferment,
But she is here, I'le leave you to your fortune.

[Enter **AURELIA MAMMON**.

AURELIA MAMMON
With me, your business?

ALWORTH
The Lady Honoria, Madam, by me humbly
Presents her service, and this paper to
Your Ladyship.

AURELIA MAMMON
The Lady Honour? 'tis
Some borrowing letter.

ALWORTH
This is not civill.

AURELIA MAMMON
I am so haunted with this mendicant
Nobility at every ebbe of fortune.
I must be troubled with Epistles from e'm.
What's here? — you are, a Scholar.

ALWORTH
I have studied the artes,

AURELIA MAMMON
Your Lady writes as much, and would commend you
To my inployment, but I want no Chaplain.

ALWORTH
If you did, I cannot flatter, Madam.

AURELIA MAMMON
I have known wiser men converted by Preferment.

ALWORTH
They were things that had no Soules,
Or use of that bright Entelecheia
Which separates them from beasts.

AURELIA MAMMON
I did expect
Hard words, and do commend the pure discretion
Of your most learned tribe, that think themselves
Brave fellowes, when they talk Greeke to a Lady;
Next to the Goth and Vandall, you shall carry
The bable from Mankind, pray tell your Lady,
Learning is out of fashion in my Family,

ALWORTH

Why should you be an Enemy to Arts?
The Lamps we wast, and watches, that consume
Our strength in noble studies, are ill paid
With this disdain, your smile would make us happy,
And with your golden beame strike new day
Through learnings universe.

AURELIA MAMMON

You but loose your time,
I know you are writing some prodigious volume
In praise of hunger, and immortall beggery.
This may in time advance you to a Pedant,
To whip the Town-top's, or gelded Vicaridge,
Some forty Markes per annum, and a Chamber-naid
Commended by your Patron.

ALWORTH

Y'are not worth
My anger, I should else—

AURELIA MAMMON

What my sweet Satyre?

ALWORTH

Present your Ladyship with a glasse, a true one.
Should turne you wild to see your owne deformity.

AURELIA MAMMON

I pretheeraile, now for a storme—

ALWORTH

I wo'not loose my temper on such a trifle.

[Exit.

[Enter **FULBANKE** and **MASLIN**.

AURELIA MAMMON

But here are two come timely, to disperse
All clowdy thoughts, my diligent daily waiters.

FULBANKE

Now Poetry be my speed! my noblest mistriss.

AURELIA MAMMON

What have you there, dear Mr. Fulbanke?

FULBANKE

Lines, that are prou'd to express your beauty, Madam.

AURELIA MAMMON

Bless me! turn'd Poet? I must tell you Servant,
Nothing in nature is more killing to me.

FULBANKE

Umh! I see my Lady Mammon is no wit.
Do'e think I made e'm? I have an Estate, Madam.

AURELIA MAMMON

I know you have fin'd for Alderman.

FULBANKE

They were a foolish Scholars o'the Town,
And I made my address to be confirm'd
In your opinion, they were wretched things,
And like the starv'd composer. The nine Muses
I have read, Madam, in a Learned Author,
Were but a knot of travailing, tawny gipsies
That liv'd by country canting, and old Songs,
And picking wormes out of fooles fingers, which
Was palmistry forsooth, and for Apollo
Whom they call'd Father, a poor silly Piper,
That kep't a thatch'd house upon Cuckolds Hill,
Not far from Helicon, or old Brideswell,
Where he sold switches, till his hut was burn'd
One night by a tinkers nose, that lay in straw there;
And he, for losse of this poor tenement,
Ran mad, from whence came all the mighty stir,
Of that, which we now call Poetick fury.

AURELIA MAMMON

'Tis very likely.

MASLIN

Madam, be your leave,
I am a country-man, what should a man lye for?
I ken no Colledge learning, but I have
Been whip'd for latin in my dayes, that have I;
And have heard talke of the Philosophers stone;
Although I weare not velvet like his worship,
My heart's imbroyder'd with love and I
Defie the man that thinkes me insufficient
To do, whats fitting to be done between
You and I Madam, as the best what lack you

Finical-fartical-citt within the walls.

FULBANKE
Take heed how you provoke me.

MASLIN
I'le provoke any man living, in the way of Love.

[Enter **PHANTASM**.

AURELIA MAMMON
Did all the Ladies sleep well?

PHANTASM
Yes and their Monkeys Madam, and have all
Their severall thanks, and services remembred
To your Ladiship— but Madam—

[Exit **AURELIA MAMMON** and **PHANTASM**.

FULBANKE
She has left us.
I'le find a time to make, you sensible—

MASLIN
Me sensible?
I defy thee.

FULBANKE
Be not rampant, and thank Heaven
We are not arm'd.

MASLIN
I scorne it.

FULBANKE
Dar'st thou meet me?

MASLIN
Yes, the next day after Simon and Iude
I dare, when all your liveries go a feasting
By water with your gally foist and pot-guns,
And Canvas Whales to Westminster I am not
Affear'd of your green Robin-hoods, that fright
With fiery club your pitifull Spectators
That take pains to be stifled, and adore
The Wolves and Camels of your company.
Next whom the children ride, who innocent things,

What with the Gyants, and the Squibs and eating
Too many sugar-plumms, take occasion to
Perfume their Pageants, which your Senators
Ride after in full scent.

FULBANKE
Thou horrid Lumpe
Of leather, course wooll, ignorance and husbandry,
Most pitifully compounded, thou that
Hast liv'd so long a dunghill, till the weeds
Had over-grown thee, and but ten yards off,
Cosen'd a horse that come to graze upon thee,
Thou miserable thing, that wert begot
By the whole Town, thou dar'st call no man Father,
Found in a hedge, but bred up in a stable,
Wherewith the horse thou did'st divide the bean's,
Dung like the beast, and wert as often curried.
Thus bred, at one and twenty thou wer't able
To write a legible Sheep's mark in tar,
And read thy own capitall letter, like a gallows
In a Cows buttock.

MASLIN
Suffer this?

FULBANKE
And more:
Fortune conspiring with thy own ill nature,
That durst be damn'd for Money, made thee rich,
And then the Countreys curses fatten'd thee,
Time, and thy sordid sins made thee at last
High-Constable, and now thou hast the impudence—

MASLIN
Thou liest.

[**MASTIN** strikes **FULBANKE**

[Enter **PHANTASM** with two Swords.

PHANTASM
Fear not me Gentlemen, I am your friend,
A friend to both your honours; here, be noble
You have a just cause, and a gallant Mistriss
Persons of your quality, to fight thus
For bloody noses, too't like Gentlemen,
And draw blood handsomely, he that gets the victory
Shall ha my Lady, and a pardon, though

It cost her half a Million, so I leave you.
Here will I stay, and observe both their valours.

FULBANKE
We are betraid.
Obscures

MASLIN
I do not like these tooles.

FULBANKE
It is not for my credit to be kill'd,
If he have but the courage to advance,
I am no Merchant-taylor of this World,
And yet he lookes less rampant. Sirrah Maslin—

MASLIN
I were best deliver up my cold iron, here.

FULBANKE
He does approach.

MASLIN
And yet I wo'not. Fulbanke.
I am of thy opinion, we are both
Betraid; for my owne part, although I carry
No flesh that feares a sword; yet I do not
Affect to have devices put upon me.

FULBANKE
Tis something thou hast said; this may be a plot;
Some third man has projected by our ruines
To make his path smooth to my Lady Mammon;
And thus her Squire promotes it.

MASLIN
A conspiracy!
I read it in the rascals face, too't quotha
Like Gentlemen no, they sha'not laugh at me.
And my Lady had a mind to ha my throat cut,
She shall excuse me.

FULBANKE
To my wishes! but
I am not satisfied,
We can without some blood come off with honour,
You know th'affront was mine, and though I wod not
Have my revenge writ in too deep a crimson,

Yet something must be done, it will be publick,
And we may still be laugh'd at.

MASLIN
Thou saist right,
Things cannot well be clear'd without some blood.
I have consider'd, and you shall be satisfied,

FULBANKE
So, I have made fine worke, the Bore will fight now.

MASLIN
The credit of a wound will serve, thus then—

FULBANKE
Stay, I have a device will bring us both off.
Why may not we consent to give each other
A careless wound in the leg, or arme, and so
March off with honour?

MASLIN
This knack was in my very thoughts, 'tis Ex'lent.

FULBANKE
But since I nam'd it first, 'tis my invention,
And I will strike the first blow.

MASLIN
Hang't, I pass not,
But gently then, a scratch ith arme, or hands
Enough, a small thing does it, gently, oh!
Thou hast cut of my Sword hand, this is fowle play,
I cannot hold my toole now.

[Drops his sword

FULBANKE
But stoope to reach it,
I'l cut thy head off, Ith field we must
Use all advantages. This weapon's mine too.
Farewell, and say I have used thee honourably.

[Enter **PHANTASM**.

PHANTASM
Ha. ha. ha. are you hurt Sir?
I see the Alderman has outwitted you.
Let me see, ha! a scratch, a very scratch;

Beare up, there may be wayes to your revenge,
Leave not your applications to my Lady.
He counsells this, that will assist you — but
I ever thought your habit much beneath
The person that should court so great a Lady.
It smells too much ot'h team: I know y'are rich.
Aire, aire your gold, and make your body clinkant,
The rest commit to fate, and me, consult
Your Taylor.

MASLIN
And my surgeon; Sir I thanke you.

PHANTASM
You do not know, how I am contriving for you.

MASLIN
That very word has cur'd me. I'le about it.

[Exit.

PHANTASM
So, when ther's no other mischief to be done,
Let them go on, and love my Lady Mammon;
I'le assist one, in hope the t'other may
Go hang himself, and then it will be hard
To judge, which of the two has the better fortune.

[Exit.

SCENE II – A Room in Honoria's House

[Enter **HONORIA** between **ALAMODE** and **COLONEL**.

ALAMODE
Bless me but with one smile, if you did know
With what devotion my Soul lookes on you,
How next to my Religion I have plac'd,
(If not above it,) your diviner beauty—

HONORIA
Your name is Alamode, a Courtier.

ALAMODE
'Tis sweetned by Honoria's breath,

COLONEL

I have
No stock of pefum'd words to court you, Madam,
Can you affect a man? A soldier?
When I have march'd upto a breach, which look'd
Like Hell with all his sulphurous flames about it;
My heart was fixt on honour, and I tooke
From gaping wounds the fleeting Soules about me
Into my owne, and fought with all their spiritis;
The mangled bodies that I trod upon,
(For now the dead had buried all the Earth)
Gave me addition to Heaven where, in,
My strong imagination I saw
Thee from thy Chariot dropping down a Garland.

HONORIA

You are a Colonel.

COLONEL

I profess a soldier Madam.

HONORIA

It appears a bold one; art thou come Alworth.

[Enter **ALWORTH**

What said the Lady Mammon?

ALAMODE

One that has some relation to her person.
They call him Alworth, and I have observ'd
She lookes on him with favour above a Servant,
He has not the impudence to court his Lady

HONORIA

So peremptory? what a strange monster wealth is?
I have but made a tryall of her friendship,
And had no meaning thou should'st leave me Alworth,
Depend upon my care, I know your parts;
And shall not be forgetfull of their merit.
But thou art come most seasonable to relieve me.

ALAMODE

I do not like their whispering.

ALWORTH

If you please, Madam, to absent your self,
Leave me to the excuse.

HONORIA
Do so, dear Alworth.

ALWORTH
I am happy when you command me service.

HONORIA
Be confident, I keep a silent register of all,
And shall reward them.

ALWORTH
Your own vertues guide you.

[Exit **HONORIA**

COLONEL
My Lady's gone.

ALWORTH
But has commanded me to let you know
Her resolution, she hath found you both
Ambitious of honour, both deserving,
And such an equall furniture of merit,
She has no art to reconcile her thoughts
Into one fortunate choice.

ALAMODE
'Tis very strange.

ALWORTH
The Gordian, which great Alexander could not
By subtilty dissolve, his sword untwisted;
I use her own words, Gentlemen, you may
Inferre, that you must either quit your courtship,
Or by your selves agree, who best deserves her,
And dare do most to merit such a mistriss.

ALAMODE
How, best deserves her?

COLONEL
And dare do most,

ALWORTH
I should interpret this to fight for Honour.
But you can best expound, and so I leave you.

[Exit.

COLONEL
What sayes my perfum'd Alamode to this?
Will not a sword quite spoile your sattin Doublet,
And let in too much aire? your lips and language
Bath'd in the oyle of Gessamine will not carry her,
You have worne a sword thus long, to shew the hilt,
Now let the blade appear.

ALAMODE
It shall. I have yet
No ague, I can looke upon your buffe,
And punto beard, yet call for no strong-water,
I am no Tavern gull, that want protection,
Whom you with oathes do mortifie and sweare
Into the payment of your ten pound surfeits;
Upon whose credit you weare belt and feather,
Top and Top-gallant. Go to your Landab—
It'h new Brothell, she's a handsome leverett,
If she deny free quarter, tear her trinkets,
Make Cullice of the Matron, yet be friends
Before the Constable come in, and runne
Ot'h ticket for the dear disease.

COLONEL
Go on sir.
I will have patience three minutes longer,
To hear thy scurrile wit, and then correct it.

ALAMODE
Answer but one coole question, if Honoria
Should possibly descend to think well of thee,
And by some philtre should be brought to love thee.
What Jointure could we make, what's the per annum?

COLONEL
Have you done yet?

ALAMODE
'Tis not impossible,
You may have a Catalogue of Town's and Leaguers
The Names of Bridges broken down, your nose
In time may keep them company in Landschape:
You will tell of Bulworkes, Barricados, Fort's.
Of outworkes, half moones, spurres, and parrapets
Of turnepikes, flankers, Cats and Counter-scarfs,
These things will hardly pawn with Jew or Christian;

But i'le come closer to you, you may have
In ready wounds some twenty, i'le admit,
And in diseases can assure her forty;
This wo'not do, she cannot eate a knapsack,
Or carry baggage, lye in your foule hutt,
And rost the pullen, for whose pretious theft,
You and the gibbet fear to be acquainted.
If you return into your wholsome Countrey,
Upon your honourable wooden legges,
The houses of Correction have but thinn
Accommodations, nor the Hospitalls.

COLONEL
It does appear by all this impudence,
And little wit pilfer'd, and put together,
You do not know me.

ALAMODE
Cry your mercie, Sir.
You are a great Field-officer, are past
These petty things, but if these times preserve
Their smooth complexion, it wo'not be
Ten hundred thousand pistols to a stiver,
But you may run this gantlope once agen.

COLONEL
You imagine you have stung me now, and that
I think my self concern'd in this keen character?
I tell thee (wretched thing,) thou doest not reach
A Soldier, 'tis a name, three Heavens above
Thy Soule to understand, and 'twere a sin
Would lessen our own worth, to make thee know it.
You are a Courtier.

ALAMODE
Very good.

COLONEL
Nay rather.
A very impious one, you shall confess it,
Or I will cut your throat, this is no canting.

ALAMODE
Very fine.

COLONEL
Nay we know you are a fine Gentleman,
A Taffata-sattin-plush-embroydered-

Lac'd-scarlet-tissue-cloath-a-bodkin devill;
Pride is thy meat and drink, thy Library,
And thy Religion, thy new clothes only
Bring thee to Church, where thou dost muster, all
The fashions, and the trinkets, to the last
New button, upon which thy conscience sits,
And as the devill guides it, dost condemne,
Or save the people, that done, not the window's
Scape thee, for thou woot quarrell with the pictures,
And find fault with the Apostles, for not having
A better Taylor, these Sir are your vertues,
Your high, and holiday devotions.
What moral vices follow in the weeke,
Is best known to the devill, your close friend,
That keeps the Catalogue, yet one touch of them;
Thy lust has no bounds, when thy blood's a fire,
Thou leap'st all like a Satyre, without difference
Of kindred, or acquaintance; and were those
But summon'd, whom thy body hath infected,
They would stuffe an Hospital, and out-stinke the Pest-house.

ALAMODE
And yet I walke upon these poor supporters.

COLONEL
How long the Chirurgeon knowes.

ALAMODE
These all my faults?

COLONEL
No, those are but thy Peccadilloes,
Thy malice is behind, thou woot not take a bribe
To undo a Nation, sell thy Countrey men
To as many persecutions, as the devill
Or Dutch men had invented at Amboyna;
With all this stock of villany, thou hast
An impudence—

ALAMODE
I'le heare no more,

COLONEL
A little i'le intreat you, all is but
A preface to your bearing, which must follow,
Your tribe will beare it.

ALAMODE

Then have at you Sir.
They make a Pass.

COLONEL
Y'are very nimble Courtier.

ALAMODE
As you see.

COLONEL
Good Mounsieur Quicksilver,
You may be fixt.

ALAMODE
And your arrear's be paid.
Another Pass, Alamode down and disarm'd.

COLONEL
What think you now?

ALAMODE
It is your fortune Sir.

COLONEL
Y'are at my mercie, aske your life?

ALAMODE
I scorne it.

COLONEL
I'le kill you then.

ALAMODE
A boy may do as much
At this advantage.

COLONEL
Will you not aske your life?

ALAMODE
No 'tis not worth it.

COLONEL
And't be not worth your asking, 'tis not Worth
My taking at this posture, there's your weapon,
Rise, use it agen.

ALAMODE

It shall be thus to render it.
Though I was not so base to beg my life,
Yet since you have given it me, I scorne to imploy it
Against one that was the master on't,

COLONEL
This is gallantry.

ALAMODE
You taught it first.

COLONEL
In spight of all the Widdowes in the World
We will be friends.

ALAMODE
I meet it Colonel.

COLONEL
And for the Lady Mammon—

ALAMODE
Wee'l take our chance.

COLONEL
A match, now let us to th' Tavern.

[Exeunt.

ACT II

SCENE I – A Room in Aurelia Mammon's House

Enter **FULBANKE** and **PHANTASM**.

PHANTASM
I Think I have brought your business we about, Sir.

FULBANKE
Thou hast oblieg'd me everlastingly:
Nay nay, be covered, thou art my best friend.

PHANTASM
It was but Justice to advance your merit
With all the Retorick I had, for where
In prudence, could my Lady Mammon place

Her self with more advantage to her fame?
A widdow of a thousand pound per annum,
With some few present bagges of musty Gold,
Old Plate, and hungry houshold-stuff would serve
The Countrey well enough.

FULBANKE
Excellent Phantasme!

PHANTASM
Where the report of building a Free-school
And now and then an alme-house for old women,
With five teeth and a half among sixteen,
Would make a mighty noise, and the poor hinds
Wonder, there's so much money left in nature.
The City is her only sphere of glory.

FULBANKE
Right, very right.

PHANTASM
Here My Lady Mammon.
Yours now as things are ordered.

FULBANKE
Good.

PHANTASM
May have high and noble waies to employ her treasures.
Do things above the vulgar admiration,
Surround the City with a wall of Silver,
Transmute dull Leaden-hall to Gold, rebuild
The great Cathedrall of St. Pauls with Porphyrie
And clap so bright a spire upon't, shall make
The Sea-man afar off wonder what new
And never setting starre, Heaven hath created
To make the day eternall in this Island.

FULBANKE
My own Phantasme.

PHANTASM
There is no end, Sir, of herwealth, if you
Have but the patience to spend, you may
Out-do the Roman Luxuries.

FULBANKE
I'l give thee my Gold-chain.

PHANTASM

O'h no, it may do you better service, Sir,
'Bout your own neck hereafter; for all this
Infinite Treasure that she brings you, Sir,
What Joynture do you make her?
You are mortall.

FULBANKE

I ha thought of that,
I will secure my whole Estate upon her?
Beside her own, I have no kindred, that
I care for, they are poor, and as my pride,
While I am living, will not look upon e'm,
At death, it will be wisdom to forget them.

PHANTASM

It would endeare my Lady much, if you
Surprize her with this act, before she think on't.
I would have you do things gallantly —

FULBANKE

You shall
Give the direction to my Counsell;

PHANTASM

His name.

FULBANKE

A very honest able eminent person,
One Mr. Traverse, see it done your self.

PHANTASM

My Lady will take it well, without all do bt, Sir.

FULBANKE

But shall I engage your trouble —

PHANTASM

'Tis an honour;
I'l give him order to dispatch all presently.
He is a very honest man you say.

FULBANKE

He's right, I know him intus & in Cute.

PHANTASM

My Lady, Sir, leave things to me.

[Enter **AURELIA MAMMON**.

FULBANKE
My most divine Aurelea!

AURELIA MAMMON
Dear Mr. Fulbanke,
I have no happiness but in your presence,
When shall the worke be perfect?

FULBANKE
I was considering,
It would become the glory of my Bride,
To have some state, and triumph at our marriage,
I know the City will expect we should
Accept some entertainment, perhaps Pageants,
And speeches to congratulate our Nuptial.

AURELIA MAMMON
'Twill please me much.

PHANTASM
There may be prejudice in these delay's,

FULBANKE
Oh Sir, the state is all; what thinks your Ladyship?
We will have tilting too, and feats of Chivalry
At Court where I'l defend my Aurelia Princess,
In the guilt armour that I mustered in,
And the rich saddle of my owne perfuming,
I'l have my squires, my plumes, and my devices,
And with my lance encounter the whole mirrour
Of Knight-hood, and compell the forreign Princes
To hang up all the Tables of their Mistrisses
As Trophee's to my most victorious Mammon.

PHANTASM
Without some cure he will be mad immediately.

[Enter **ALAMODE**, reading a Letter, a **SERVANT** waits.

ALAMODE
Present my humblest service to Honoria,
Say I am all obedience to her commands,
Were I in Heaven, this invitation
Would have the power to draw me thence, I kiss
Her fairest hand, this for your favour,

[Gives him money.

Mr. Fulbanke,

FULBANKE
Please you to know my Lady Sir?

ALAMODE
If I mistake not the Lady Aurelia;
Widdow to the late high Treasurer, Sir
Omnipotent Mammon.
Salutes her?
But are you Master of this rich Peru?

FULBANKE
She will please to owne me, Ha!

AURELIA MAMMON
It is but Justice.

ALAMODE
A thousand streams of joy flow in your bosoms,
I'l take some fortunate hour to visit you,
And with an humble lip print my devotions
On your white hand.

AURELIA MAMMON
You'l do me an honour sir.

ALAMODE
Some high affairs compell this rude departure,
But you have mercy to excuse your servant.

[Exit.

FULBANKE
What heaps of words some men have got together
To signifie nothing?

PHANTASM
How do you like this Gentleman?

FULBANKE
These Courtiers are another sort of flesh-flies,
That haunt our City dames, but we must winke,
Or loose our Chatter?

PHANTASM
Bless the Body Politick.

[Enter **MASLIN** in rich Cloths, but Antick.

MASLIN
By your leave Gentlemen.

FULBANKE
What Pageant's this?

MASLIN
Where De'e think I have been, Madam?

MASLIN
At the Brokers.

MASLIN
At the Exchange by these silke-stockings,
Mr. Usher—a word to the wise,
If they will fit your rowling pin, they'r paid for;
Perhaps the wages you receive in your
Relation to my Lady, wo'not find you
Convenient vanities. Now I'me for you Madam.

AURELIA MAMMON
In good time.

MASLIN
I wanted but your hand,
I could ha fitted you with gloves, but here are
Some trifles for the finger, you must weare
This Diamond, and this Ruby,

AURELIA MAMMON
De'e understand
What you do sir?

MASLIN
And here's a casting Net of Pearl.

AURELIA MAMMON
A Carkanet? these will deserve—

MASLIN
Tell not me of desert, I hate it perfectly,
Hang toyes and yellow rubbish that paid for e'm,
How De'e like my clothes?

FULBANKE
Sir I am concern'd to thank you for these favours.

MASLIN
You? prethee away, I ha nothing to say to thee?

FULBANKE
We have no other gratitude sweet-heart,
But to invite him to our wedding.

MASLIN
Wedding? Phantasme.

PHANTASM
And you had come but half an hour sooner,
This very shape had don't.

MASLIN
Do not, do not make me mad too soone.

FULBANKE
You have been very bountifull, and we pray
Your noble presence at our Festivall,
Which we have deferr'd to be attended with
Some Triumph, such as may become the City,
And my dear Ladies honour, is't not so,
My America? look how the oyster gapes.
Leave him to chew his Countrey cud, come Madam.

[Exeunt.

PHANTASM
Sir I confess.—

MASLIN
And be hang'd, I am undone, and I could cry now.

PHANTASM
Sir,
You have been at a great charge to go without her,
Such rings, and Carknet, beside the cost
Of this fine habit? for your bounty, Sir,
Bestowed on me, the unworthiest of your Servants,
I have a gratitude, if you please to accept it.

MASLIN
What is't? a halter or a knife to cute me,

Or a comfortable poison?

PHANTASM
'Tis the first
You nam'd, a most convenient, neatly twisted
Halter, for I do see your inclinations,
And shall commend your fortidude, beside
'Twill shew a brave contempt upon their scorns.
And who know's, how the example, Sir, may spread
To cure some other mad men that love widdows.
You have my judgement and the cord for nothing,
Lose not the nick of the next beam you come at,
No way like this to be High-Constable.

MASLIN
Here, take my clothes; I will be mad, and hang
My self immediately; — and yet I will consider,
Till the ayre be a little warmer; when I have
Cut Fulbanks throat, 'tis but a hanging afterwards.
'Tis good to be malicious, and wise;
Some notable revenge would be worth all
My cost, and then a sico for the Devill.

[Exit.

SCENE II – A Room in Honoria's house

A table with a cabinet upon it.

[Enter **ALWORTH** and **ALAMODE**,

ALWORTH
Please you to have a little patience
I shall acquaint my Lady that y'are come, Sir.

ALAMODE
Before you go, dear Sir, I know your prudence
And neere imployment with my Lady, has
Endeer'd you to part ake some of her Counsells;
You shall obliege a very humble Servant,
To let me know how she affects, you reach
My meaning, by what motive am I sent for?

ALWORTH
My Lady keeps the key of her own Cabinet,
But if you'l have my Judgement on the scheme,

I think my Lady will this day determine
Her choice, I encline the rather to this Judgement,
Because the Colonell is sent for too.
My attendance is expected, Sir, your pardon.

ALAMODE
Ha musick.
A song within praise of a Courtier.
I like this well

[Enter **COLONEL** and **ALWORTH**.

ALWORTH
My Lady will appear presently,
I'l give her knowledge, if you please.

COLONEL
Your favour, Sir,
You are learned beyond books, what's your opinion
Of my Lady, in relation to things at present?
What do you think of me?

ALWORTH
My thoughts are much
Too narrow to conclude your worth, which left
An object for Divine Honoria's wisdom,
Must only take from her, a worthy character
And just reward.

[A song in praise of a Soldier.

COLONEL
I like this preface.

ALAMODE
My noble Colonell, thy Servant.

[Enter **HONORIA** attended, a Table set forth, with a Cabinet upon it.

HONORIA
Excuse the trouble that I give you Gentlemen,
Y'are welcome, and thus knit into a freindship,
Your persons have more grace, and shine upon e'm.
Some chairs, pray sit. I see you both preserve
Your fair respects to honour, and I have
After some pause, and serious dispute
Within my self, collected now at last,
Upon whose person to repose my self,

My fortune, and my same, and since but one
(Where many may deserve) can weare the Garland
The loser must content himself with his fate,
And wait a kinder providence.

COLONEL
'Tis but Justice.
She takes a wreath of Bayes from the Cabinet.

HONORIA
This wreath of bayes, embleme of victory,
Must crowne his head to whom I fall a Conquest,
Forgive the Ceremony.

COLONEL
Oh 'tis very pleasing,

ALAMODE
I like it well, Madam, and commend your fancy.

HONORIA
You, Sir, were bred up in the Schoole of honour,
The Court, this may not unbecome your Temples,
Wise Courtiers are the Jewels of a Crown,
The Columnes and the ornaments of state,
Fitted with parts; and piety to act:
They serve the Power for Justice, not themselves;
Their Faith the Cabinet, in which is laid
The Princes safety, and the Nations peace,
The Oracles, and the mysteries of Empire;
Men borne above the fordid guilt of avarice,
Free as the mountain aire, and calme as mercy.
Borne without Eyes, when the poor man complains
Against the great oppressor, without hands,
To take the bloudy price of mans undoing,
But keeping at each sense a Court of Guard,
Draws fear from Love, and teaches good by example.
She puts the Wreath upon the Colonell.

ALAMODE
Divine Honoria.

HONORIA
You must give me leave,
To try, how it becomes his brow; me thinks
With the same grace, in dwells upon his head,
Does he not look like mighty Iulius now,
When he returned triumphant from the Gaules,

Or bringing home the wealthy spoiles of Egypt,
Pontus, and Africa, allow him but
The same commands, and men to fight, why may not
His Valour equall what is fam'd in story,
Archiev'd by the great souls of Rome, and Carthage?
A soldier merits first to be called man,
By whom not only Courts but Kingdoms flourish,
Unto whose severall offices, the World
Owes all the great and glorious names of honour.
How would the age grow rusty, and the soule
Of Common-wealths corrupt with ease, and surfeits,
Should not the sword call e'm to exercise,
And sweat out their unmanly Luxuries,
By acting things worth envy, even of Princes.
The honour of the Gowne without his sword,
Will run it self into contempt, and Laws
Are not good made, but while the sword secures e'm.
The Court must weare no silke, nor the prowd City
Make the Sea groane with burden of her wealth,
Did not the active soldier, with expence
Of his dear blood, expose himself abroad,
Their convoy, and security at home.

COLONEL
I am transported.

HONORIA
Give me the same favour
To let me looke a little on this Chaplet,
To which I have annexed my self a Labell.
Me thinks the Trifle looks, as it had lost
Some Verdure since I took it from your heads,
The Courtier, and the Soldier both inviting
In such a high degree of merit, hinders
The progress I should make, but pardon me,
I shall soone quit the Labarynth.

COLONEL
What's the meaning?

HONORIA
I would you were not two, or that one had
Less of desert, when you are both in ballance,
Have you no art, Gentlemen, to contract
Your selves into one person?

ALAMODE
'Tis not possible.

HONORIA
Think you so? it is worth the experiment,
Come hither Alworth.

ALWORTH
Madam.

HONORIA
Nay come nearer,
This is a Scholar, Gentlemen, and the cloud
He weares, remov'd, for he's no more a Servant,
May bring him into a civill competition:
Me thinks it fits him, your opinion?

COLONEL
We are in a fair way to be ridiculous, what think you?
Chiaus'd by a Scholar?

ALAMODE
Are you in earnest Madam?

HONORIA
I repent not
The placing of it there, in him do meet
The Courtier and the Soldier, at least
He's not without the best capacity
Of both your worths, when they have brightest lustre.

ALAMODE
There is no remedy.
Would I had Mammon.

HONORIA
Gentlemen stay, & hear the Scholars character.

COLONEL
No thank you Madam, we have heard too much,
Fortune has given you Lawrell, and us willow.
May your wreath flourish, Sir?

[Exeunt.

ALAMODE
Soule of my muse! what active unknown fire
Already doth thy Delphick wreath inspire?
O'th suddain how my faculties swell high,
And I am all a powerfull Prophecie.

Sleep ye dull Caesars, Rome will boast in vain
Your glorious Triumphs, one is in my brain
Great, as all theirs, and circled with thy bayes,
My thoughts take Empire ore all Land, and Seas.
Proof against all the Planets, and the stroke
Of Thunder, I rise up Augustus Oake,
Within my guard of Lawrell, and made free
From age, look fresh still, as my Daphnean tree:
My fancy's narrow yet, till I create
For thee another World, and in a state
As free as innocence, shame all Poets wit,
To climb no higher than Elizium yet;
Where the pale Lovers meet, and teach the groves
To sigh, and sing bold legends of their Loves.
We will have other flights, and tast such things
Are only fit for sainted Queens and Kings.
All that was Earth falls of, my spirits free,
I have nothing left now, but my Soule and thee.
Honoria takes off the Wreath.

HONORIA
What means this Extasie? this was not meant,
Unless you use my favours with less insolence,
I can repent, and frowne e'm back to nothing.
Have you forgot your distance? can a smile
And this green trifle forfeit your discretion,
Or make me less, than when you were my Servant
I look you should be humble still,

ALWORTH
Good Heaven!
What unexpected, most prodigious cloud,
With his black wings, hath in a minute veild
The brightest day, that ever smil'd upon me?
Did not you place it here?

HONORIA
It is confest,
As an encouragement to your vertue, Sir,
No Conquest of Honoria, yet you triumph,
And make me blush as I had courted you.

ALWORTH
O do not charge my thoughts with such a stain,
This might deserve your anger, and vouchsafe me
The boldness to say Madam, if you punish
My hasty application of your favours,
You gave me the encouragement to be guilty.

It is a tyrany to cherish Servants,
And punish their obedience.

HONORIA
But when flattered by
Pride, which darkes the soule, you challenge
And measure the reward by your own fancy,
You loose the noblest recompence of service,
And merit but the hire of common duties;
'Tis possible, that Gold may satisfie
My debt to your imployment.

ALWORTH
Till this minute
I was not lost, but having heard this, Madam,
You must do something like a miracle
To save me now;— I dare contemne your Gold,
And am compell'd to ask your Justice, what
Action since I had reference to honour,
Look'd with a mercenary staine upon it?
Gold is a pay for soules of darke complexion.
I served you for your self, and since I'm thought
Beneath the merit of your smile, I'l make
My self above the price of sordid contracts,
For I can with as much ease despise your wealth,
As I can shift the ayre, I take my leave,
And can pray for you in a Wilderness.

HONORIA
Come back, this minute every cloud is vanish'd
That did present displeasing formes: I find
Thy soule is pure, forgive this Triall, thou hast
Deserved me best.

ALWORTH
I dare not understand you now.

HONORIA
The language is not hard.

ALWORTH
I want a name, to call this blessing by,
Then I may kiss your hand, and may I not,
Madam approach your lip, and be forgiven?
Now I begin to doubt.

HONORIA
My Faith?

ALWORTH
That I am not awake, or if I be
That I am short-liv'd, and must soone dissolve
Under this storme of happiness; Ha! 'tis come
And I have lost my courage o' the suddain.

[Faints.

Your pardon Madam, something gathers here
That wo'd surprize my heart. I am asham'd on't.

[Enter **SERVANT**.

HONORIA
Who waits, contribute your best help to his
Support, convey him gently to his chamber,
Run for Phisitians, thy good genius guard thee.

ALWORTH
I am not Worth your fears.

HONORIA
And worth my love?

ALWORTH
That very word should cure me,

HONORIA
I have been
Too much, I fear unkind, to both our dangers.

[Exeunt.

ACT III

SCENE I – A Room in Traverse's House

A table with with bottles and glasses.

TRAVERSE, seated at his table, **DASH** attending.

TRAVERSE
Wait at the door, my Clients are so numerous
And pressing with their suites, they almost stifle me.
Let me enjoy the aire of my owne Chamber;

I think I have lost some lungs in the last cause.
Let me indulge a little to repair e'm,
A glass of the Greeke wine, Th' Italian Merchant
Presented me, and let the Terme go on,
I'l drive the Law at leisure, and o're take it.
Clarke fills Wine into the glass.
So so, this looks sprightly,
Be carefull of this Treasure, 'tis my blood,
Wast not one drop, upon thy life I charge thee.
Dash drinks from the bottle.

DASH
Wast quothe?
You shall not prove a wast, I'l warrant you.

TRAVERSE
So, so, remove.

DASH
Sir your Idolaters, the Writs are come.

[Enter **WRITS**.

TRAVERSE
The weather's hot, let no more spirits enter,
Now like the soveraigne Bee, methinks I sit
On my prodigious hive, surveying all
By wing'd, industrious people, bringing honey,
And making wax more pretious than a trade
To both the Indies. My good Emissaries,
And faithfull spirits of the Law, descend
To your infernall shades, untill I call you,

[Exeunt **WRITS**.

[Enter **DASH**.

DASH
A Gentleman desires to speak with you Sir,
From the Lady Mammon.

TRAVERSE
Admit him.

[Enter **PHANTASM**.

DASH
What a fine thing this Terme is?

And what an ungodly time, the long Vacation?

PHANTASM
Sir, I'l not hold you long, I know you have business,
There have past some overtures of love and marriage,
Between your City Client, Mr. Fulbank,
And the Mistriss that I serve, the Lady Mammon.
And you should draw a Deed to settle on her
His whole Estate, if she survive, as Joynture—

TRAVERSE
I understand you Sir.

PHANTASM
I am glad you do, this Sir is his desire,
And to have all dispatch'd with expedition.

TRAVERSE
Very well.

PHANTASM
But the reason of my coming is
To desire you sir, to let all this
Alone, there is another thing, that will
Concern you more materially.

TRAVERSE
Your meaning?

PHANTASM
You are not married.

TRAVERSE
I enjoy a freedom.

PHANTASM
My Lady Mammon has a vast Estate,
And is a widdow, you do understand?

TRAVERSE
Her name is precicus to the World.

PHANTASM
The World's an asse, you look like wiseman,
You have a good face, and a handsome person
Under a Gowne, you have a good Estate too;
I am a Servant, that have credit with her,
By my relation; and I have no mind,

The City Mule, your Client, should breake
His back with burden of his gold; in short,
I wish you well, and if you have the confidence
To make a motion for your self, this high
And mighty widdow, may be yours; I'm plain.

TRAVERSE
Say you so?

PHANTASM
I'l bring her to you, and prepare her too,
Have I been tedious sir,

TRAVERSE
My better Angell!

PHANTASM
Legions attend my Lady, trouble not
Your head why all this kindness from a stranger.
I had a revelation to do thus;
Have a strong faith, and think upon't, your Servant.
If within half an hour she visit you,
Think it no dreame, and thank me afterwards,
Now leave your wonder, and be wise.

TRAVERSE
Can this be true? 'tis not impossible.
This is a pretty vision would I had her.
If she appear I may believe, and prosper.

[Enter **MASLIN**.

DASH
The tide is coming in,
Mr. Maslin the High-Constable, a good man
And full of causes.

TRAVERSE
What intrusion's this?

MASLIN
I have given a sop to Cerberus your doorkeeper.

TRAVERSE
O' Mr. Maslin you are become a stranger.

MASLIN
'Tis not for want of love to be at Law.

Your worship knows, I am apt to trouble you,
And the whole County where I live.

TRAVERSE
Your business?

MASLIN
Sir, it is extraordinary, and I desire
Beside your learned worships fees, to pay
For expedition.

TRAVERSE
You speak reason.

MASLIN
I do abound in reason, look you Sir

[Shews Gold

'Tis all of this complexion; here's a piece
For every day till the next Terme begin,
And two for every day it lasts.

TRAVERSE
Have a care of your health, good Sir;

MASLIN
And you of your spectacles.

TRAVERSE
What must I do for this?

MASLIN
Do? you must undoe
A friend of mine.

TRAVERSE
A Friend?

MASLIN
We are all friends in Law, Sir,
Never did man suffer so fast an injury,
And therefore take him to your legall malice.

TRAVERSE
Has he kill'd your Father?

MASLIN

Worse, worse:

TRAVERSE
Made a whore of your sister?

MASLIN
Worse than that:

TRAVERSE
Ravish'd your wife?

MASLIN
Worse than all that, and yet this comes the neerest,
He's cheated me of my wench; a widdow Sir
That has more money than all your profession
Has got, since the dissolution of the Abbeys.
In short, this is the Case, Fulbanke, the City
Gulfe has swallowed my Lady Aurelia Mammon.

TRAVERSE
O Caniball!

MASLIN
Devour'd my widdow, wife
That should ha been, this man I hate, this man
Must be undone, and there's part of the money.

TRAVERSE
The Lady Aurelia Mammon?

MASLIN
That very Polcat; but I must tell you Sir,
They are not married yet, if you have now
A dainty Devill to forbid the banes—

TRAVERSE
Although this be a case, more pertinent
To the Court Ecclesiasticall, yet,
Let me consult my Law-giver.
Turns his Books.

MASLIN
Sir, so I may
Be reveng'd, I stand not much upon't,
Who has this Mammon, let the Devill take her,
Or your worship take her, 'tis all one to me.

TRAVERSE

Hum! I shall stretch a point of Law for you.
You shall have your desire, I do expect
Her presence instantly,

MASLIN

Is that a conjuring book, expect her instantly?
Now i'le pronounce you master of your wishes,
For you shall have—

MASLIN

The widdow?

TRAVERSE

What is sweeter than the widdow,
You Sir, shall have revenge, and Mr. Maslin
To vex him more, de'e observe I will have the widdow, My self.

MASLIN

You will, and what shall I have?

TRAVERSE

Sir, you shall have revenge, revenge, the joy
Of flesh and blood, life and delight of nature,
The poor mans Luxury, and the rich mans bath,
Above all wealth or widdows Sir. Mr. Maslin,
I'l tame his blood, and his Estate by Law,
While you shall crack your spleen with mirth and laughter,
And wonder at my subtill arts to vex him.

MASLIN

All this is reason.

TRAVERSE

This shall be done by Law for the High-Constable.

[Enter **MAMMON** and **PHANTASM**.

MASLIN

The Lady's come; this Gentleman
Has studied the black art.

TRAVERSE

Do you withdraw, and leave me opportunity
To wind the widdow up.

MASLIN

Behind the Hangings;
He obscures.

[**PHANTASM** exit.

TRAVERSE
Vouchsafe your Servant touch your hand, your lip
Is an ambition more becoming Princes:

AURELIA MAMMON
I am not proud, where fair salutes invite me.
I come to give you a little trouble, Sir.

TRAVERSE
Madam command me, to the extent of all
My faculties.

MASLIN
His faculties? that will carry her,
She is a glittering fairye, but he'le conjure her.
Stay if he takes this prize, what shall have
For all my expences! that's considerable;
Oh, I shall have revenge he says; the widdow
Were much the better but we must be rul'd
By our learned Counsell.

AURELIA MAMMON
You have order from
A Gentleman of the City, Mr. Fulbanke,
To draw up writings, sir—

TRAVERSE
A Joynture Madam.
But I receiv'd a Countermand.

AURELIA MAMMON
From whom?

TRAVERSE
From providence that would not suffer such
An excellent Lady to be lost, and thrown
Among the City rubbish.

AURELIA MAMMON
Do you know Mr. Fulbanke Sir?

TRAVERSE
As much, as I do wonder at his impudence,
And sawcy ambition with his mean deserts
To look at such a blessing; your fortunes

Are worth your preservation, and a man
Whose art, and serious knowledge in the World
May fence it in from a rapine, and that greater
Enemy to an Estate, profusion.
Excuse my plainess Madam.

AURELIA MAMMON
'Tis a Truth.

TRAVERSE
Can you vouchsafe your smile upon a Servant,
To whose faith and care you safely may commit
A Treasure of more value than the World,
Your self; in me behold him Madam, one
That would devote his soule a Sacrifice
To be for ever burning in those beams,
There is no Law, but in your breast, your lips,
Preserve the Nations Oracle.

AURELIA MAMMON
This Language
Doth tast too much of Poetry, take heed, Sir.

TRAVERSE
If this dislike you Madam, I can court you
In a more legall way, and in the name
Of Love and Law arrest you, thus

[Embraces her.

AURELIA MAMMON
Arrest me?

TRAVERSE
And hold you fast imprisoned in my arms,
Without or baile or maineprize.

AURELIA MAMMON
This does well.

TRAVERSE
I can do better yet, and put in such
A declaration, Madam, as shall startle
Your merriest blood

AURELIA MAMMON
I may put in my answer.

TRAVERSE
Then comes my replication, to which
You may rejoyne, Currat Lex. shall we?
Joyne issue presently?

AURELIA MAMMON
He'l have her,
Se defendendo.

[Enter **PHANTASM** and **FULBANKE**.

PHANTASM
What do you think of this, Sir?

FULBANKE
They are very familiar.

MASLIN
'Tis he, the very he, come as my heart
Could wish to his vexation.

PHANTASM
Is this the honest Gentleman
You trusted, Sir;

TRAVERSE
Who attends?

[Enter the **WRITS**.

FULBANKE
My passion stifles me.

MASLIN
Are you come
My delicate Devills cut in way? let him not
Approach too near, he can take measure
Of his forehead at this distance.

PHANTASM
These were my fears, marriage had made sure worke,
I was against your stay for tilts, and triumphs.

AURELIA MAMMON
'Tis Mr. Fulbanke.

FULBANKE
Would any strumpet vex an honest man thus?

AURELIA MAMMON
Strumpet; you shall have suell to this jealousie.

MASLIN
Excellent Pidgeons! admirable Spiders! ha, ha, ha.

FULBANKE
I'l be revenged.

TRAVERSE
Currat Lex.

PHANTASM
Excuse me, Sir, I must follow the Law,

[Exeunt.

[The **WRITS** enclose **FULBANKE**.

MASLIN
Joy Mr. Fulbanke, and a whole bundle of babies ha, ha, ha.
Your wedding day was notably deferr'd
To be attended with more Ceremony,
And such an anti-masque of sucking Devills.
He looks like the py'd Piper in Germany,
That undertook to cure the Town of Rats,
And now the fry of Vermin dance about him.
I am left to chew my Countrey cud, an asse,
A ridden-empty-pated-sordid Coxcomb:
You do command in chief o're Cuckolds sconce
Or Haven, to which all the Tups strike saile,
And bow in homage to your Soveraigne Antlers.
Most high and mighty halfe moon, Prince of Becos.
And so I kiss your hoof.

[Exeunt **MASLIN** and **WRITS**.

FULBANKE
Well; if there be money and malice in the City,
Expect a black revenge upon ye all.

[Exit.

SCENE II – A Room in Aurelia Mammon's House

[Enter **PHANTASM**.

PHANTASM
My nimble Lawyer thinks he has got my Lady,
And hugges his happiness, my next worke shall be
To spoile his practice, mischief is my office.

[Enter **ALAMODE**.

Most noble Alamode,

ALAMODE
My old acquaintance?

PHANTASM
I am proud that you will owne me, Sir, your Creature.

ALAMODE
When is this day of Triumph in the City.
For high and mighty Fulbanke, and your Ladies
So much expected marriage?

PHANTASM
At the Greeke Calends;
My Lady's has left the Alderman allready.
He may now change his Heraldry, and give
In's coat an armed beast at the new bull-ring
In a field dirt.

ALAMODE
whether is she gone prethee?

PHANTASM
To Travers sir, who has yet no Terme for life.
Your hopes thrive I guess in the fair Honoria.

ALAMODE
She's a haggard too.

PHANTASM
Possible?

ALAMODE
She has gull'd us learnedly,
And took the Scholar, in few months you'le heare
Her brought to bed of Philosophy, she's gone,
And I may as soone hope to reprive thy Lady,

PHANTASM
My Lady? with your pardon, gentle sir,
Can you find in your self any warme thought,
Or meaning to my Lady?

ALAMODE
Could I wish
To live, and look at happiness?

PHANTASM
You have been a noble Patron to me.

ALAMODE
What canst thou do?

PHANTASM
Do, I can do the office of a Gentleman,
And you shall go your part, and perhaps owner.

ALAMODE
Make me so happy.

PHANTASM
I'l conduct you,
You come i'th opportunity.

[Exeunt.

SCENE III – A Room in Traverse's House

[Enter **TRAVERSE**.

TRAVERSE
My starres conspire to make me a full happiness,
Since, fame spread my intended marriage
With Lady Mammon, methinks the people
Look on me with another face of feare,
And admiration, in my thoughts I see
My self allready in the Throne of Law,
In which the petty purples waite, dispersing
As I incline to frowne, or smile, the fate
Of trembling mortalls,

[Enter **PHANTASM**.

PHANTASM

He is return'd.

TRAVERSE
Where is thy Lady, thou art (I observe) her favourite.
And must be mine;

PHANTASM
She's in her Chamber sir.

TRAVERSE
Come I will have it so, thou art too humble,

PHANTASM
'Tis a becoming Duty, My ambition
Will be to observe the wonder of your happiness,
And how you'l rise to greatness, and to glory,
By matching with my Lady,

TRAVERSE
You are not
A stranger to her closset, it will be
An engagement to acquaint me with her temper.

PHANTASM
She is a woman, Sir, but you are wise.

TRAVERSE
Nay, nay, I must know her nature.

PHANTASM
'Tis very gentle, she is angell Gold,
And you may bend her as you please, she is
A teeming Lady too.

TRAVERSE
What Children?

PHANTASM
All provided for, they'l not trouble you,
She has a thousand friends.

TRAVERSE
Thou art kind, proceed—

PHANTASM
You are a Gentleman,
Whose wisdome I may trust, I should not use
This freedom else.

TRAVERSE
Thou maist tell me any thing.

PHANTASM
She loves to be abroad, and to disperse
Her shine upon some persons that adore her,
That's all her fault, she wo'not be confind, Sir;
And how the softness of your nature will
Consent, to keep her under lock and key—

TRAVERSE
Umh! if she be so volatile, I must
Hang weight upon her, 'twill be necessary.

[Enter a **DOCTOR**.

Retain thy wisdom and observe my Lady,

PHANTASM
It is my duty, Sir.

TRAVERSE
My noble Client.

DOCTOR
I ha not leisure to aske how go causes.

TRAVERSE
Yours will be heard, the first day of the Term.

DOCTOR
I build upon your care.

TRAVERSE
You may be confident,
Neglect my Doctor, to whose care, and art
I owe my lungs, and life?

DOCTOR
Oh you are pleasant,
But I am now engag'd, and shall desire
I may be excus'd, you know my Lady Honoria

TRAVERSE
She is not sick.

DOCTOR

No, but a Gentleman
Whom she declares most precious to her, is,
(I'th height of expectation, and fair hopes
To have been her husband,) desperately falne Sick,
And now I think on't, 'tis my wonder, you
Made no addresses timely to that Lady.
Men that are eminent in Law, are wont
To be ambitious of Honour.

TRAVERSE
Oh Sir
It is a maxime in our politicks,
A Judge destroyes a mighty practiser.
When they grow rich, and lazie, they are ripe
For honour.

DOCTOR
You have Sir a swelling fortune.

TRAVERSE
I have Mammon, I think, and for my owne part
Can easily consent to accept of Lordship.

DOCTOR
If this man take the toy, and dye, she's worth
Your thoughts, my learned in the Laws, I wish
Sir I could serve you.

TRAVERSE
Nay, nay prethee Doctor.

DOCTOR
The Gentleman may suffer,

TRAVERSE
If he dye,
You and I shall be friends, i'le not engage you
To poison him.

DOCTOR
You have more justice.

TRAVERSE
Yet I should not breake my heart, if he were dead,
And the faire Lady mine, I know not, but
This very mention of her, at this nick
Of time, when her delight is taking leave,
Hath a strange operation in my fancye:

You know my constitution, I may want
Your ay'd, but honourably.

DOCTOR
You shall command it.

TRAVERSE
Then i'l to her instantly, and beare you company.

DOCTOR
You can pretend no visit, being a stranger.

TRAVERSE
No, I will go under the notion of
Your friend, and fellow Doctor, one o'th Colledge.

DOCTOR
You may do so.

TRAVERSE
I need not shift my habit.

DOCTOR
And what then?

TRAVERSE
Observe, and see the Motions of my Lady,
Who knows but I may feel her'pulse? I prophecie
Something will follow fortunate. If I thrive
Thou shalt be King of Cos, my learn'd Hyppocrates
And I will be thy Servant.

DOCTOR
'Tis too early to court her.

TRAVERSE
'Tis a fault of modesty
In men to think so. Women are no fools,
And howsoe're they bridle it, 'tis providence
'T entertain new comforts, I have heard
A modest Gentleman say, that made his love
Known to a Lady e're her husbands flesh
Was cold i'th crust, I meane new cofind up,
But he had a repulse, the answer was
He came too late, the widdow had been promis'd
The day before.

DOCTOR

If you be so resolv'd,
I'le waite upon you, Sir:

TRAVERSE
The rest to my kind starres, come wee'l take Coach.

[Exit.

[Enter **AURELIA MAMMON, ALAMODE** and **PHANTASM.**

AURELIA MAMMON
Presume to lock me up? thou ha'st my Jewells.
I'l leave him instantly.

ALAMODE
He fears his tenure,
And would secure your Ladyship from starting,
But this doth very well become your prudence,
To quit the house e're he improve his interest,
By some new quirk in Law.

PHANTASM
A noble Gentleman!
And one that honours you religiously.

AURELIA MAMMON
You much obliege me sir, and I look on, you
Design'd by providence my preserver; wee'le
Into t'h Countrey instantly.

ALAMODE
Any whether, excellent Phantasme!
I am your Servant Madam, to wait on you
Through the World.

PHANTASM
I was borne to make you—
A foole, or I am mistaken.

[Enter **DASH.**

This is his Clarke, and spie upon your person.

ALAMODE

How the rascall squints upon us?

AURELIA MAMMON
Tell Mr. Travers,
The Bird is flowne, commend me to his night-cap,
I shanot see him till the next vacation,
So farewell penny a sheet.

ALAMODE
And dost heare? bid him
Provide new locks and keys, and barres and bolts,
And cap the Chimney, least my Lady fly
Out at the Lover hole, so commend us to
The precious owle your Master.

[They kick **DASH**.

PHANTASM
One token from me.

[Exeunt.

DASH
You have trusted me with tokens of remembrance,
I would my Master had received them in
His propria persona, to have thank'd you.
Their toes are somewhat harder than my haunches;
But this is nothing to the generall damage,
If our great Lady Mammon be run from us;
Which I believe, as sure, as I am waking,
And have been kick'd, the most convincing argument.
All our hopes come to this? our mighty hopes
Huge as a Mountain, shrunke into a wart?
We are undone, and may go hang our selves.

[Exit.

SCENE V – A Room in Honoria's House

[Enter **HONORIA**.

HONORIA
I was too blame, my curiosity
Now suffers for the Triall of his vertue;
And he too apprehensive, when I chid
The Ambition of his love, made himself past

The cure of my affection.

[Enter **DOCTOR** and **TRAVERSE**.

Sir, you are welcome:

DOCTOR
Madam, I presum'd
To bring another able Doctor with me
For his consult, in case there may be danger.

HONORIA
You have very much oblieged me.

TRAVERSE
She is a very gallant Lady!
Inspight of all the clouds that dwell upon her.

HONORIA
Who waits there?

[Enter **SERVANT**.

Shew these Doctors Mr. Alworths
Chamber, there is another Gentleman within
Of your profession; your cares shall find
A gratitude becoming both my self,
And your owne worth, and I may tell you Doctor,
If it may give the least addition to
Your Cheerfulness, in his you will preserve my life.

DOCTOR
Madam, retain but your own vertues, and be confident.

HONORIA
Poor Alworth, there is left no other way
To pay my satisfaction to thy merits,
But with my sorrow for thy sufferings,
And what will be thought pious to thy memory,
Of Fate translate thee hence: ha, he is returned.

[Enter **TRAVERSE**.

What think you Sir?

TRAVERSE
I wish he could sleep Madam, I am for his sleep,
It would be a benefit, truth is, I much fear him

But 'tis not prudence (give me boldness Madam)
To let this Sorrow play too much a Tyrant
On your fair cheek: This shews him precious to you,
If the Srars envying his converse on Earth,
Court him to their bright Dwellings, you must be
Arm'd with a noble Fortitude, and consent
To let him rise a Constellation there,
And not impair your self, who were not meant
To be snatch'd hence, by over-hasty sorrow,
But live the worlds best Ornament.

HONORIA
Did you say
That sleep would much advantage him? What think you
Of some soft murmures of the Lute, or Voyce?
I have heard the purlings of a spring will make
Our senses glide into a dream I have a Page did use
To please him much.

[Exit **HONORIA**

[Enter **DOCTOR**.

DOCTOR
What think you on her?

TRAVERSE
I think? I cannot think too much upon her.
But I'll not leave her thus, her very presence
Is able to recover him.

DOCTOR
Let me tell you Sir,
I finde no Danger in him, be then counsel'd
Not to betray your self, you finde his temper
Not apt for your design, Expect a time—

TRAVERSE
I love her infinitely. Mammon is a Blouze,
A deformed Gypsie, didst ere see her Doctor?
She paints abominably, ey'd like a Tumbler,
Her Nose has all the colours of the Rainbow,
Her Lips are blue, and her teeth straddle, you
May pick'em with a bed-staff.

DOCTOR
You describe
An Elegant person.

TRAVERSE
But Honoria
Has all perfections. Stay, what fees de'e think
I have had of you since our acquaintance, there's
A purse of gold—no ceremony, I am still
In thy arrears for bringing me to see
This wonder of her sex.

DOCTOR
You are not wilde.

TRAVERSE
Your cause shall cost you nothing too, that ended,
Quarrel with all the Countrey, your Law's paid for.
Serve me but now, I'll be thy slave for ever.

[Exit.

DOCTOR
I now suspect the Lawyer is short liv'd,
Men of his Robe are seldom guilty of
These restitutions, but who can help it?
If I knew any handsome way to serve him,
He has oblig'd me.

[Exit.

[Musick, a Song.

[Enter **DOCTOR**.

DOCTOR
He'l shame us all,
He's zealously perswading the poor Gentleman
To dye with all speed, and tells him stories
Of Heaven, what a fine place it is, and what
Excellent company the Angels are;
What a base Prison to a noble Soul
The world is, nothing right under the Moon,
Or worth a manly thought; and presently
He courts my Lady, and falls into such raptures
In her commendation. The Gentleman
(Whose Crisis is not desperate, if I
Have any Judgement) smiles at his folly.
They'r both here.

[Enter **TRAVERSE** and **HONORIA**.

TRAVERSE
He's a Gentleman, whose condition,
And as he has relation to your favours,
May invite some passion: But you are wiset
Then to condemn your self to solitude,
And for his absence to despise mankinde;
Be just for your own sake, and Madam, look
Beyond his Hearse, with pitty on the living,
'Mongst which, you cannot want, as just admirers,
And some that may be worth your second thoughts.

HONORIA
What mean you Sir?

TRAVERSE
I mean your second choice.

HONORIA
This language makes your Charity suspected.

DOCTOR
You are too violent, leave us a while.

[Exit **TRAVERSE**.

HONORIA
Your friend is full of counsel.

DOCTOR
You have goodnes,
To place an innocent sense upon his language,
I know he has much honour to your person,
And 'tis sometimes as necessary, to
Advise the living to preserve their health,
Which their immoderate sorrows would consume,
As cure the languishing patient.

[Enter **TRAVERSE** hastily.

TRAVERSE
Now Madam,
Your grief is useless to him, he is dead.

HONORIA
Dead?

DOCTOR

She Faints.

TRAVERSE
A blessed Opportunity!
There is a Coach at door will hold us all,
My dearest Esculapian, help, and finde
A bounty will deserve it.
They carry in Honoria.

ACT IV

SCENE I – The Street Before Traverse's House

Enter **TRAVERSE**.

TRAVERSE
I Have secur'd the person of Honoria,
At my Mannor in the Countrey, who believes
Her Alworth dead, and must be allowed some time
For that digestion. I have made known
My self, and the affection which engag'd me.
But though my Lady Mammon have a place
Beneath her in my thoughts; on better counsel,
I think it wisdom to preserve my interest
In her, already mine by her consent,
And the great plea of Law, Possession.
If I can make the Lady Honoria sure,
She shall be my wife, and that my Concubine,
Rare, Excellent!

[Enter **DASH**.

DASH
Oh Sir, y'are welcome home.

TRAVERSE
Thou look'st with a warp'd face.

DASH
You can resolve me,
Is there no case, wherein a man, without
Impeachment to his Credit or his Conscience,
May be allowed to hang himself?

TRAVERSE
What's the matter?

Thou art not desperate?

DASH
I know not, but
I finde some inclinations to Hemp.
You are my Master, I may be concern'd
To follow a good example.

TRAVERSE
Leave your fooling,
How does my Lady Mammon?

DASH
There's the business.
My Lady Mammon is Sir—

TRAVERSE
What, what is she?

DASH
She is my Lady Mammon, yet I lye,
She is not mine, I would she were your Worships,
I know you will be mad, but it must out,
My Ladies gone.

TRAVERSE
Ha!

DASH
Run quite away Sir,
With a glib Gentleman came to visit her,
And the young spirit that did wait upon her.
Without much ceremony, she would have your Worship
Provide more locks, and keys, and bars, and bolts.
I tell you Sir, Verbatim, for a need
I have it all in pedescript.

TRAVERSE
Mammon gone?

DASH
What think you Sir, of a ne Exeat Regnum?

TRAVERSE
Gone? my vexation? no pursuit will reach her,
Give her the start, and she'll out-strip the Devil.
These things will turn me wild, but that's no cure,
I must be a man agen, and tame this passion,

Her loss may have recompence, if Honoria
Can yet be gain'd, my hopes are full of blossom,
I'll return instantly, come you along Sir.

[Enter **MEN** carrying burthens of Money.

What are these? Ha! 'tis money, whence I pray
Comes all this Treasure?

1ST MAN
From the City Sir.

TRAVERSE
But whether goes it?

1ST MAN
Do you not observe
Us march in rank and file, this money goes
To maintain many honest Gentlemen
That want it, that will fight, and do fine things
For all our goods; you are a fool I see,
And do not know the Law.

TRAVERSE.
What Law?

1ST MAN.
Club Law.

TRAVERSE
How's that?

1ST MAN
The Cannon Law, do I speak loud enough?
The Gentlemen behinde will tell you more.

[Enter **FULBANKE** and **CITIZENS**, other **MEN** waiting with Bags of money.

TRAVERSE
I like not this: let us to horse immediately.

[Exit.

FULBANKE
'Tis high time, that we tame the insolence,
Of this long Robe, these Princes of the Law
Will invade all our Liberties and Fortunes.

1ST CITIZEN
Presume to take our Lady Mammon from us?

FULBANKE
And as I hear, she's closely hurried
To a Castle in the Countrey, made a Prisoner.

2ND CITIZEN
I should consent the City be still great,
And our names spread, like our ambitions,
But we not prudently consider, whom
We trust with our revenge—

FULBANKE
Our Mercenaries,
Who findes 'em buff, and iron, and when they
Come lame and halting home, who shall provide 'em
Good Hospitals, and old shirts to make lint on?
When we please, we can scatter all the Regiments
If we but rein our purses.

1ST CITIZEN
I am clear
There is no other way to carry on
The work, the sword strikes Terrour, and who knows,
The body of the Law being vast, and powerful,
Might (if not timely thus prevented) raise
Considerable strength and opposition.
But thus we stifle all, and having once
Recovered Mammon, we are Princes.

OMNES
Princes!

[Enter **COLONEL**, and **CAPTAIN SQUANDERBAG**.

SQUANDERBAG
Where shall we dine Colonel? I ha lost
My credit at the Ordinary, this Town
I think is onely scituate to starve in.
What are these?

COLONEL
They have City faces.

SQUANDERBAG
And are a thought too handsome to be Serjeants,
They have serious eyes upon us, and move to us.

COLONEL
Would you with me Gentlemen?

FULBANKE
Yes Sir, with you.

2ND CITIZEN
May I take boldness Sir, to ask your name?

SQUANDERBAG
My name?

2ND CITIZEN
For no harm Sir, you are a Soldier,
And I presume have had commands.

SQUANDERBAG
What then Sir, keep off.

2ND CITIZEN
I come in friendship, and mean all
Civilities to your person: De'e want money?

SQUANDERBAG
Would you have your pate broke?
For such a foolish question to a Gentleman?
I do want money Sir, you wo'not furnish me.

2ND CITIZEN
Do not mistake your self, come hither sirrah,
Will this do you much harm?

SQUANDERBAG
Harm! pray be covered. Miracles! De'e know
What you have done?

2ND CITIZEN
An act of Justice,
To call it Charity, would stain your honour,
I look for no security.

SQUANDERBAG
Not a note under my hand never to pay you,
What must I do for all this Sir? whose throat
Would you have cut now? these fine Devils
Must do something.

2ND CITIZEN
Buy you new cloathes, a better sword
The Leather of your boots are of two families,
You may want linnen too, get fresh, and part
With bosom friends.

SQUANDERBAG
I have more stowage.

2ND CITIZEN
And I'll employ it, at your service Sir,
He gives him another bag.

SQUANDERBAG
What will become of me?

2ND CITIZEN
Nay Sir, I must tell you,
Y'are like to have more of this.

SQUANDERBAG
Has he no cloven foot?
This is the rarest Citizen!

[Enter **COLONEL, FULBANKE**.

2ND CITIZEN.
De'e hear Sir?
We are making of our Will, and in the humour
That now predominates, that Gentleman
May be the Cities heir.

SQUANDERBAG
Were it not pity this should be a dream now?

FULBANKE
You have commission, and full instructions,
Be sure you do not pinch to spare our purses,
Our Money grows, we are fain to weed the silver,
Our men are rank, and rot upon the stalk
For want of cutting, every drum-stick is
A Lime-twig, they are mad for innovations,
Pray know my brother Sir.
Salute

COLONEL
I am his faithful servant.

2ND CITIZEN

One of the Birds, that keep the Capitol,
Our feathers are all at your service Gentlemen,
When you have pluck'd and pick'd us well, you may
Give order for our roasting, we are tame Sir.

SQUANDERBAG

Beshrew me an understanding fellow.

FULBANKE

We have no more to say, 'tis the Publique cause,
Bring Mammon home, and we will rout the Laws.

1ST CITIZEN

And so we'll pray for you.

COLONEL

For your selves Gentlemen, I do conceive
We shall do well enough.

[Exeunt **FULBANKE & CITIZENS**

Captain Squanderbag,
What think you of this change? silver comes in
Upon us like a Sea.

SQUANDERBAG

An ebb must be expected, I hate naturally
This mettal of the Moon, 'tis a pale flood,
Would I were in Pactolus streams, or Tagus,
There were a lasting Element.

COLONEL

What do you
Think of these Golden Images?

SQUANDERBAG

I honour the bright sons of Sol.

COLONEL

Pity these Gentlemen should want Civil War,
They take such pains, and pay so heartily,
We have much to do o'th sudden.

SQUANDERBAG

This long peace
Hath made us tame i'th world, let e'm now pay 'fort.

COLONEL
We are emergent from our shades, let's rise.
With subtil motion, treasure makes men wise.

[Exeunt.

SCENE II – The Country – Maslin's House

[Enter **PHANTASM, MASLIN, CONTREY-MEN.**

PHANTASM
She has gull'd the Lawyer too.

MASLIN
Most excellent,
I do adore her wit, and will she visit
The Countrey, Ha! come neerer,

PHANTASM
I have repented Sir, my past neglect?
And made this satisfaction by my Counsel,
Which has prevail'd, and now she comes to you Sir,
With pure affection to your self, the Lady
Mammon is onely yours.

MASLIN
Did you hear that?
The Empress of the world is coming hither
To me, with pure affection to my person,
We are her Vassals.

PHANTASM
'Cause the times are dangerous
Sir, she comes private, but one Gentleman
That knows not her design, I ever thought
You were born to be a great man.

MASLIN
We'll go forth to meet her.

PHANTASM
By no means Sir, 'twas her desire,
You should be onely thus prepar'd, I'll tell her.

[Exit **PHANTASM**

MASLIN

'Tis my happiness,
Shall I be at last a Dominus fac totum?
There's Latin for you Neighbours, I am inspir'd
With Languages, with all things, and you shall,
The poorest Copiholder of my Tenants
Be allow'd a Concubine.

1ST CONTREY-MEN.

Whaw! then we shall
Be Turks Sir.

MASLIN

Turks? the Turks a Civil Gentleman.

2ND CONTREY-MEN.

But no Christiam.

MASLIN

Ye'e are a fool, we
Must all come to't if the times hold, and my
Deer Mammon stay with us.

1ST CONTREY-MEN.

Bless me a Turk!

4TH CONTREY-MEN.

Is that such a matter; why you, and I,
And the best on us, are but Turks, if you
Take us one way.

1ST CONTREY-MEN.

I grant, as we are brethren, and
Turks, another way, and worse—

MASLIN

Let me see, how shall I consume my wealth?

1ST CONTREY-MEN.

What think you of building Sir a Church?

MASLIN

A Church? and give it my own name to save
A Consecration, No, no, I must do
Something to shame the Chronicles—silence,
I'll build another Town in every County,
In midst of that, a most magnificent Colledge,
To entertain men of most eminent wit,

To invent new Religions.

1ST CONTREY-MEN.
That were excellent, we want Religion extreamly.

MASLIN
Can none of you invent? I think I must
Keep men in pension to project me ways
To spend my gold.

2ND CONTREY-MEN.
Pave all the high-way with't,
'Twould be excellent for Travellers.

MASLIN
I'll pave a street, that shall run cross the Island,
From Sea to Sea, with Pearl build a bridge
From Dover Cliff to Callis.

1ST CONTREY-MEN.
A Draw-bridge?

4TH CONTREY-MEN.
This may be done, but I am of opinion
We shan'ot live to see't.

MASLIN
'Twon'ot be want of money, but of time,
Meer time, to finish it; my Lady Mammon,
Believe it, can do all things; for your parts,
But think what you would have, I say no more:
If she smile but upon you, you are made,
And may go sleep, and when you wake, run mad
With telling of your money—Ha! 'tis she.

[Enter **AURELIA MAMMON, ALAMODE** and **PHANTASM.**

I Charge you kneel, and kiss her hand,
My Lady Mammon!

ALAMODE
How's this?

MASLIN
Welcome to my heart, Madam.

ALAMODE
Is my Lady in earnest?

AURELIA MAMMON
You have done me Sir a favour, I'm at home,
And disingage your further service; I
Wish you a fair retreat.

ALAMODE
Do you hear Madam?
You will not thus reward me, after all
My travel and attendance?

AURELIA MAMMON
'Tis my meaning,
Nor will it Sir, be safe to lose much time,
These have a natural antipathy
To men of your fine making.

PHANTASM
'Tis Alamode the Courtier,
Whom my Lady has onely made her property,
To be part of her convoy.

ALAMODE
You wo'not marry him?

AURELIA MAMMON
I think I sha'll not,
I must not be confin'd, while there is ayr,
And men to change.

MASLIN
How Master Courtier?

PHANTASM
They'l toss him in a blanket.

MASLIN
As long as you please Madam, he's welcome,
And he shall eat, if you frown, he must vanish,
Or I have Canibals that will devour him;
With his sword, boots treble tann'd and spurs upon 'em.

ALAMODE
Sure I dream, but Madam
You wo'not play the Cockatrice thus wo'me.

AURELIA MAMMON
If you will stay, upon your good behaviour;

I may dispense some private favour—

ALAMODE
Good, excellent Whore, I'll stay to observe her humor.

MASLIN
I'll be your guide Madam,
On, go before, and bid'm ring the bells,
For bonefires, 'twill be time enough at night
To burn up all the Villages about us.

ALAMODE
Indeed it shall be yours: Sir, you are too civil.

[Exeunt.

SCENE III – The Same – Traverse's House

[Enter **TRAVERSE** and **DASH** the Clark.

TRAVERSE
Intreat my Lady hither, and attend her,
I did embrace too much, Mammon is lost,
If my stars prosper my ambition
To Honoria, I forgive their future influence.
A Discovery of Treasures and Iewels.
Here is a blaze to melt a frozen soul.

[Enter **HONORIA**.

HONORIA
What is my gaolers pleasure with his Prisoner?

TRAVERSE
That character doth wound your servant, Madam,
I am your Prisoner, by the fate of Love,
Condemnd to everlasting chains, my heart
Consumes at every frown, and I beg now
Not to be happy owner of that beauty,
Since you decree my Exile, but to dye,
Collect up so much terrour in a look,
And from that Throne of Majestie, your eyes,
Dart forth a flame of wrath so high, it may
Turn me to ashes, I'll submit your Sacrifice.

HONORIA

I have no thoughts so impious, to destroy
A life that may be happy, if you be not
Your own Tormenter.

TRAVERSE
Those words have a sound of mercy, Madam.

HONORIA
Cruelty and honour
Are inconsistent.

TRAVERSE
I taste Heaven,
Already, a warm stream descends upon
My timorous heart; Oh pause, let me consider
How much I am behinde in worth, to know
What change hath blest it.

HONORIA
Change?

TRAVERSE
Let me but touch
Your white hand, were my breath the Treasure
Of all the East, no other Altar should
Have Incense, I am lost to finde the sweetness.

[Salutes her.

For every smile I drop a Pearl, these Diamonds
Are pale, and beg a lustre from your Eyes,
Wear them, and be their ornament: I'll rifle
My Indies for more wealth, and when I have,
With giving up my soul, purchas'd a kiss
Of bright Honoria, from my dust at one,
One pittying look upon me, I ascend
A new Creation from your Eye.

HONORIA
What means
This rapture? what would all this passionate noise?
Expound, I am still Honoria.

TRAVERSE
Oh say but mine.

HONORIA
Sir, shut up your shop,

Your gay temptations wo'not take.

TRAVERSE
Is't possible?
Not all this treasure buy one kiss?

HONORIA
A thousand,
From those that have a subtil art to sell them:
Why do you trifle with your soul? Intents
That carry honour, need not bribe with wealth
To purchase nothing.

TRAVERSE
I can love you vertuously.

HONORIA
By that love be commanded then, to tell me
How have you dispos'd of Alworths dust, why was I
Surpris'd dishonourably, and transported
Against my own thoughts and consent, to this
Unhappy place? and immut'd up like
Some guilty person, not allow'd the freedom
Of ayr, nor to see heaven at all, but from
The narrow limits of a Cazement? can you
Interpret this affection? 'tis tyrannie,
That must without a penitence, draw from heaven
A justice, and from me (by you made miserable)
A just contempt of all your flatteries.

TRAVERSE
There are some men i'th world, that would not think
You handsom in that look, and make you tremble.

HONORIA
You dare not be so impious.

TRAVERSE
When my love,
That courts you honourably is scorn'd, I can
Be angry, had I wanton thoughts about me,
As some may mix with flesh and blood, you are
Within my power.

HONORIA
That power is circumscrib'd,
You have confin'd already this poor weight
Of Dust I carry, but if blacker thoughts

Tempt you to force my honour, I can call
Rescue from heaven.

TRAVERSE

What needs this bravery? you see I use
No violence, I court you to a Bride.

HONORIA

My vows once gave me up a pledge to Alworth,
And my heart cut out for his Epitaph,
Will not contain one Character beside.

TRAVERSE

I play my self to death in flames unpittied,
Resolve, nor look for tedious considerings;
If I may honourably succeed your Alworth,
His soul had not a purer faith to serve you,
If this be slighted—

[Enter **DASH** the Clark.

DASH

Help, help, we are all undone, O Sir, where is
Your two handed sword?

TRAVERSE

Thou Messenger of Horror, what's the matter?

DASH

The Castle is besieg'd, and the Beacons burns blue Sir.
The Devil's up in Arms, and comes against us
With the whole posse Comitatus! they
Will pull the house down they have broke into
The base Court, Heaven protect my Pia mater.
I did but peep out of the Garrat, and
One Soldier swore a huge Granado at me.
They cry down with the Laws, and if they have not
Honoria sound of wind and limb, they'll cut us,
Sir, into Labels. Would I had compounded
For any leg or my left arm; but now,
Now farewel comely Court-hand, and long Dashes,
Do you not hear the Mandrakes? what do you do Sir?
I'll into the Cellar straight, and bar the door,
And if there be no remedy, e're they reach me,
I'll drink, and dye a Martyr.

TRAVERSE

I am blasted! stay,

There is a close contrivement in this Chamber,
Madam, will you retreat, and save your person?
This way sirrah.

[Exeunt.

DASH.
De'e think they will not smell us out? I fear
My constitution wo'not hold.

[**SOLDIERS** within.

Down with the Laws & custos Rotulorum,
Fico for Writs and Mous-Traps.

[Enter **OFFICERS, GENERAL**, and **FULBANKE**.

OFFICER
Make a guard Soldiers.

FULBANKE
I am come Sir, to see fashions.

COLONEL
You finde us drudging Sir, in your affairs,
Captain, I leave him to your entertainment,
That face deserves a reverence.

HONORIA
'Tis the Colonel,
But he looks more compos'd, and carries state.

COLONEL
Madam.

FULBANKE
And how go things, my Military friends?
My gallant men of action? you are now
In sprightly postures, and become your selves,
What pitty 'tis, men of your noble soul
Should want employment.

SQUANDERBAG
We must all acknowledge
Your care of us.

FULBANKE
I honour'd your profession,

Since I first handled Arms.

SQUANDERBAG
What service, with your favour have you seen?

FULBANKE
Hot service, I was knock'd down thrice, and lost
My beard at taking of a Fort in Finsbury,
And when I had my Marshal trinkets on,
I thought my self as brave a Macedonian
As the best on e'm. But where's the Lady Mammon?

COLONEL
Surprized? and ever since a Prisoner?
He is not worth my passion, this room
Has in your presence a protection.
I take your word, you wo'not quit the place
Without your servants knowledge, Madam, but
If the slie Enemy of your honour, think
By obscuring his base head, to fly our Justice,
When you are safe, I'll fire the house upon him.

DASH
Here, here we are, fire, fire.

TRAVERSE
Be silent Villain.

DASH
Yes, and be burnt alive, I cannot finde the door.

COLONEL
From whence that voice?

DASH
'Tis here, 'tis here, I hate burning, as
I do the Devil, and a dry Proverb, help.

SQUANDERBAG
The Lawyers here.

TRAVERSE
Gentlemen use no violence, I'll come forth
And meet your fury.

CAPTAIN
What are you sirrah?

DASH
A poor Court-hand practiser.

CAPTAIN
The choice is given, whether thou wilt be hang'd
At the next tree, or have your ears cut off?

DASH
My ears, my ears by any means Gentlemen
Hanging will make a villainous long Dash.
Once crop'd, and twice a Traytor, sweet Gentlemen,
Delicate Commanders.

TRAVERSE
Time has brought
Your turn about, by your respects to honour,
I see your soul is noble; though I cannot
Dye at my own choice, I can make a will,
And dispose some Legacies, rich Jewels, Sir,
Plate, Gold, and Silver.

FULBANKE
All this I lay claim to,
They were the Lady Mammons, in whose right
I challenge all, I take those to my custodie.

COLONEL
How? How? Marshal take him to yours.

FULBANKE
Me to the Marshal? that were pretty, me?

MARSHAL
Come Sir—

FULBANKE
How? I beseech one word, have you forgot me Sir?

COLONEL
Your name is Fulbank.

FULBANKE
Plain Fulbank? it was I,
Did in those days bring in the good advance.

COLONEL
You did, your duty Marshall—

FULBANKE
I ha done Sir,

COLONEL
So have not I, secure his person too,
Safe, as your life will answer it.

[Enter one with a Letter.

Letters, whence? Ha!
From Alamode?

[He reads.

[**ALWORTH** Discovers himself to **HONORIA, SQUANDERBAG** observes them.

He writes where a party of horse may handsomely
Secure the Lady Mammon, give him a reward,
Make it your province Captain, you will finde
Directions in that paper. [Whispers].

SQUANDERBAG
Sir, I have observ'd
That Gentleman with the black-patch uncase
His eye once to my Lady, there's some mysterie,
I do not like it.

COLONEL
Some spie: when I walk off, command him to the
Guard till further order.
Madam, I call it my first happiness,
That I am in a capacity to serve you,
And you shall order your own justice.

HONORIA
What will they do with that young Gentleman?

COLONEL
She mindes not me.

HONORIA
Your pardon.

COLONEL
Give me favour to attend you,
With whom my soul desires to be renew'd,
Your faithful honourer, march on.

[Exit **COLONEL** &c.

ALWORTH
I obey you.

SQUANDERBAG
You will know the cause hereafter, and us better,
When both your eyes are open.

[Pulls of the Patch.

CAPTAIN
Thou hast cur'd him: de'e know us Sir?

ALWORTH
I know ye all.

SQUANDERBAG
What are we?

ALWORTH
You're all close fires, in want of aire kept tame,
But know no bounds, let loose into a flame.

SQUANDERBAG
We'll teach you better Morals Sir, Come on.

[Exeunt **OMNES**.

ACT V

SCENE I – Metropolis – A Guard Room

Enter **SQUANDERBAG** and a **CAPTAIN**.

CAPTAIN
HIs thoughts are all now taken up with Courtship
To Honoria.

SQUANDERBAG
You may see Captain,
A handsome piece of flesh and blood may do much,
When there's no other enemy i'th field.

CAPTAIN
What will be done with the Gentleman was carried

To the guard?

SQUANDERBAG
The stranger with a black Eye?
He's fast enough, and will have opportunity
Of place and time, to cool his hot devotions,
If our Commander in chief march on thus.

[Enter **SERJEANT** and **SOLDIERS**.

SERJEANT
Are not these pretty hand Granado's, Gentlemen?

1ST SOLDIER
Fire to the fuze, and toss some health about.

2ND SOLIDER
Come away, tomy Colonel, honest Squanderbag.

SQUANDERBAG
Ha! these are my Scythians, mark those fellows Captain,
Cut'em in pieces like so many Adders,
They'l joyn agen, i'ch compass of an acre,
Their limbs will creep together, and march on
To the next Rendevouz without a halt.

2ND SERJEANT
This is Spanish.

SERJEANT
Draw home your arrow to the head, my Centaure.

1ST SOLDIER
Mine is French Wine.

5TH SOLDIER
You must take your chance,
The Yeoman of the wine-seller did not
Provide'em for our palate.

2ND SOLDIER
Supernaculum!
See, there lies Spain already, now would I fight—

SERJEANT
Drink thou mean'st.

2ND SOLDIER

With any King in Europe.
Do not spill your Amunition; ah Serjeant,
This was excellent Drink.

1ST SOLDIER
Who wants my Colonel?

2ND SOLDIER
I want it, tope, give me't.

SERJEANT
He'l ha't agen?

2ND SOLDIER
The to'ther charge, and then we'll over-run
Christendom, Sa, sa:
When y'ave done with Christendome, what shall
Become o'th Heathen Princes?

2ND SOLDIER
We'll put the Heathen Princes in a bag.

SERJEANT
A bottle thou meanest, he's all for drink.

2ND SOLDIER
And after, roast the Great Turk with his Bashaws,
Like a pudding in's belly.

SQUANDERBAG
Thou Boy!

1st SOLDIER
There he is for eating.

SERGEANT
Dost know what thou hast said now? but
What shall be done with the Jews?

2ND SOLDIER.
They are included,
And go upon the score of Modern Christians,
There sha'not a Nation scape us.

SQUANDERBAG
These are the men,
The tools, that cut our Triumph out o'th quarry.

CAPTAIN
They will deserve their pay.

SQUANDERBAG
Oh pay is necessary, use it now and then,
Like Phisick, it keeps the Soldier in health
And expectation, they must fight for honour
Some-times.

1ST SOLDIER
Tobacco, hey?

SERJEANT
Here boys, a Magazine, with pipes attending,
White as my Ladies tooth, and shining more
Then forehead of Dulcinea de Toboso.

4TH SOLDIER
A Soldier's a brave life.

3RD SOLDIER
'Tis cheap, all these things come to us by nature.

SERGEANT
Our Colonel.

SQUANDERBAG
I'll cashier him that rises, keep your postures,
We are all Soldiers, and can sit and drink we'e,
To your Arms Gentlemen agen, Ha! this is wine.

SERGEANT
We have the modest gift of drinking, Sir,
Without inquiry of the Grape or Vintage,
Or from what Merchant.

SQUANDERBAG
Is not this better than a tedious Prentiship,
Bound by Indentures to a shop and drudgerie,
Watching the Rats, and Customers by Owl light?
Ti'd to perpetual language of, What lack ye?
Which you pronounce, as ye had been taught like starlings.
If any Gudgin bite to damn your souls
For less than sixpence in the pound. Oh base!
Your glittering shoes, long graces, and short meals,
Expecting but the comfortable hour
Of eight a clock, and the hot Pippin-pies,
To make your mouth up? all the day not suffered

To aire your selves, unless your minikin Mistress
Command you to attend her to a Christning,
To bring home plums, for which they may relieve
Your teeth that water, with her next suppositorie.
You have some Festivals, I confess, but when
They happen, you run wilde to the next Village,
Conspire a knot, and club your groats apiece
For Cream and Prunes, not daring to be drunk,
Nothing of honour done, now y'are Gentlemen,
And in a capacitie to be all Commanders, if you dare fight,

2nd SOLDIER
Fight? you know we dare, Sir,
And with the Devil.

SQUANDERBAG
In hope you wo'not give him quarter,
There's money, do not purchase Earth, nor Heaven with it.
I must away, remember the two things.

1st SOLDIER
The two Dees.

SQUANDERBAG
Drink, and your Duty, so,
Now as you were—

2nd SOLDIER
Noble Colonel,

[Exit.

Let me kiss thy hand, I am thine body and soul.

3rd SOLDIER
But will you fight with the Devil?

2nd SOLDIER
Why not?

3rd SOLDIER
So will not I.

2nd SOLDIER
Wo'not you fight with the Devil, and one of
Our Regiment?

3rd SOLDIER

Not I?

1ˢᵗ SOLDIER
Perhaps the Devil is his friend.

3ʳᵈ SOLDIER
And yet in a good cause—

2ⁿᵈ SOLDIER
He wo'not fight with you then, base, I say,
To take advantage of the cause, or person:
Fight upon any cause with any person.
Heark you Serjeant, you do know our Duties
Better than we our selves, what do we fight for!
Silence the first word of Command, let us
Be serious, what, what do we fight for?

SERJEANT
For pay, for pay, my Bull-rooks.

2ⁿᵈ SOLDIER
La'ye now,
Can any Christian Officer say more?

SERJEANT
Hang these Intergatories,
And give us to'her charge to'th man i'th Moon.

2ⁿᵈ SOLDIER
All, all give fire together, Oh for a noise
Of Trumpets.

[Drums beat.

1ˢᵗ SOLDIER
Here are Drums.

SERJEANT
The General is coming this way, to your Arms
Skud ye Metropolites.

[Enter **COLONEL, SQUANDERBAG, CAPTAIN** and **ALAMODE**.

ALAMODE
Sir, I congratulate your honourable
Employment.

COLONEL

And I your noble presence here.

ALAMODE
I could not with my Rhetorick invite
My Ladie hither?

COLONEL
I sent you a party—

ALAMODE
Yes Sir,
Your men of rank and file do carry still
The strong perswasions, they prevail'd with her.
I left her to the Guard.

[A shout.

COLONEL
The reason of that Clamor?

CAPTAIN
The Soldiers, Sir, express their joy thus loud,
That Ladie Mammon is brought in, the Guard
Hardly secure her person.

COLONEL
Give her fair access,
On pain of death, be none uncivil to her,
This service will deserve a memory,
And publique thanks, all our design did reach
But to gain her.

ALAMODE
The work will be to keep her,
The Gipsie has more windings than a Serpent
The Moon is not more changing.

[Enter **AURELIA MAMMON, PHANTASM, GUARD.**

COLONEL
Is this she?

PHANTASM
Madam, I'll take my leave.

AURELIA MAMMON
Forsake me in this
Condition?

PHANTASM
If I could expect a worse
Would fall upon you, Madam, I'd not part yet.

AURELIA MAMMON
How?

PHANTASM
For I can tell you, what will follow instantly,
And it does please my wickedness extreamly,
The next pay-day you will be torn in pieces,
Oh'twill be excellent sport, ha, ha, ha.

AURELIA MAMMON
And canst thou laugh Villain? Secure him Soldiers.

PHANTASM
They will have work enough about your Ladiship.
I am going as nimbly as a spirit, Madam,
And to your greater comfort, know I am one.

AURELIA MAMMON
The Devil thou art.

PHANTASM
Call'd by another name,
Your evil Genius, to assure you that
You have been all this while cozened, my dear Mistress,
And that these colours are phantastick, see,
I vansh into aire.

GUARD
Presto, was this your Devil, Madam?

AURELIA MAMMON
Oh my misfortune!

COLONEL
Madam, your person is most welcome hither.

AURELIA MAMMON
I fear your Soldiers, Sir,

COLONEL
You may be confident
Of safety from them, Madam, that fight for you,
We are your guard, all wait upon my Ladie,

And let your applications be with reverence,
And see her entertainments high, and such
As may become my honour, and her person.

[Exit.

What is there left addition to my happiness?
Mammon and Honoria both within my power?
Ambition write non ultra, fix, fix here,
The two great darlings of mankinde are mine,
Both Excellent, and yet but one Divine.
Wealth is the nerves of War and Wit, without which
We are dull, and useless engines, Mammon leads
To Conquest, and rewards our blood and watches
But honour is the lustre of all Triumph,
The Glories that we wear are dim without her,
Till she come in, the Lamp, our glorious flame,
We grope our way i'th dark, and walk on crutches.
Riches may shine, and Star-like grace the night,
But Honour is the radiant soul of light.

[Exit.

SCENE II - A Prison

Enter **ALWORTH**

ALWORTH
I almost could be angry with my fate,
And call that care of my Phisitian
Unkinde, that did remove my first distempers;
I should have drop'd into the shades, and lost
Her memory, that flatters me to ruined
What's all this murmure? are these thoughts my own?
Or is there some black spirit crept into
My melancholy blood, that would corrupt
That spring, by which my innocence should live?
Hence, I command thee hence, thou dire Inchantment,
And let the vertues of Honoria
Resume their throne within my soul, and strike
Religious tremblings through every thought,
Lest I repine at Providence? She is here.

[Enter **HONORIA**, and **MARSHAL**.

MARSHAL

This warrant must admit you.

HONORIA
There's for your Office, you may withdraw your self.

MARSHAL
Your servant.

[Exit.

HONORIA
Oh my Alworth?

ALWORTH
This humility
Transcends my hope and merit, I am now
No more a Prisoner, since my better part
(Enlarg'd by this your charitable visit)
Hath freedom to behold my greatest happiness,
Your self.

HONORIA
I am so full of joy
To see thee alive, I cannot ask thee, how
Thou wert preserv'd.

ALWORTH
Heaven was not willing I
Should die, till I had given you better proof
How much I would deserve your smile upon me.

[Enter **COLONEL** and **MARSHAL**.

MARSHAL
Here you may, undiscovered, Sir, observe 'em.

COLONEL
You may be gone, and wait at some fit distance.

ALWORTH
My cure was hastned by your thoughts upon me,
And my desires had wings to reach your person,
(For I was soon acquainted how you were
Convey'd) and next my thoughts to kiss your hands,
I brought my resolutions of revenge
Upon that Traitors head, that ravish'd ye
So rudelie from my eies.

HONORIA

Prethee no more,
But let our hearts renew, and seal a contract
In spight of present storms; and I am not
Without some hopes to change thy sad condition,
For he, to whose commands thou owest this misery
Is pleas'd to say he loves me, and I can
Employ his kindeness to no better use
Then thy Enlargement; if this prove unfortunate,
It shall at least diminish thy affliction,
That I can bear a part, and suffer with thee.

ALWORTH

Better I sink by many deaths, then you
Engage your self to any unkinde Fate
For me; I have crept newly from my dust,
And can alone walk cheerfully to silence
And the dark grave: But do you believe, Madam,
This man looks on you with a noble flame?
He's now a great man.

HONORIA

His affection
Has all the shews of honour, and such high
Civilities flow from him.

ALWORTH

Pause a little,
And give me leave to tell you, as these seeds
Of War grow up, I cannot think a person
(Though many may be honourable) can
Better Deserve—

HONORIA

What?

ALWORTH

To be made Lord of this
Fair Empire.

HONORIA

Did this language come from Alworth?
That said he lov'd me?

ALWORTH

Yes, with noblest fervor,
My love commands it Madam, and I can
In my true service to Honoria,

Advise her to call home her noble beams,
Thar shine to the discredit of her light
On me, that would upon a worthier object
Draw up more admiration to her brightness,
And at the same time, by their influence shew
The beauties of her better choice.

HONORIA
This language
I understand not yet; can Alworth then
Finde in his heart any consent, to give up
His interest in Honoria to another?

ALWORTH
Yes, when Honoria is concern'd to meet
A greater happiness than Alworth, I
Can make my self an Exile, which is but
The justice of my love to her great merit.
I am a trifle Madam, a thing meant
Beneath your smile, a very walking shadow,
And time will come, when you have shew'd me all
The bounties of your grace, nay seal'd them mine,
By the most holy character of marriage,
Yet then I must forsake you, when my nerves
Shrink up, when the weak flowings of my blood
Cool in their channel, and tame Nature leaves me
A spoil to death—

HONORIA
Why do you talk of death,
So far off?

ALWORTH
Though we do not hear him tread,
Yet every minute he approaches, Madam;
And give me leave to tell you, without flattering
My self, I am in danger; first a Prisoner,
A spie they may pretend, but this will vanish.
It is the title of your servant, Madam,
Is both my hononr, and my crime, nor can I
Wave my relation to your favours: this
Known to the man, under whose power we stand,
His angrie breath may doom me to the scaffold,
And I must then resign, nor will the act
Be mine, but a constraint, and I then lose
The glorie that may now be mine, to engage
Him in your smiles, you in his love.

HONORIA

When will this dream be over?

ALWORTH

As for me,
It shall be enough at distance to look on you
With thoughts as innocent as your own, and if
For the convenience of both our persons,
One Earth must not contain us, do not think
That I can wander, where I shall forget
To tell the stranger world your storie, Madam;
And when I have made all mankinde, where I come,
Bow to your name, and taught 'em to repeat it
In all their dangers, and their frights, to cure them,
I will seek out some aire, that is infectious,
Where no birds dare inhabit, or man build.
A cottage to repose his wearied head,
And there I prophesie, by the vertuous charm.
Of your blest name, to purge it, and as soon
As the great miracle is spread, to invite
The best of every Nation to live there,
And own you Tutelar Angel.

HONORIA

Fie, no more,
Alworth now dreams indeed, but he more vainlie
Perswades me to forget my vows to him:
Is this a fear to die, or something like it?
For I would give it fain some other name.

ALWORTH

A fear to die, that arrow strikes too deep,
If you but think so, and wounds more than all
The horror my destruction can appear in.
If I can entertain the thoughts of life
Without you, how much easier must it be
To die for your concernment? I ha' not liv'd
After the rate to fear another world.
We come from nothing into life, a time
We measure with a short breath, and that often
Made tedious too, with our own cares that fill it,
Which like so many Atomes in a Sun-beam,
But crowd and justle one another. All,
From the adored Purple to the Hair-cloth,
Must center in a shade, and they that have
Their vertues to wait on'm, bravely mock
The rugged storms, that so much fright 'em here,
When their souls lanch by death into a sea

That's ever calm.

HONORIA
This deserves my attention,
And you in this small lecture Alworth, have
Made me in love with death, who for thy sake
Can with my innocence about me, take
More satisfaction to bleed away
My life, than keep it, with the smallest stain
Upon my honour. This I speak, not to
Court up your drooping thoughts to me, if I
Be faln, or have lost my first esteem—

ALWORTH
Oh pardon, t'other syllable of this destroys me;
What is there, can but make me worthy of
Your faith? I am all, ever thine? The Colonel.

[Enter **COLONEL**.

COLONEL
Expect a cloud to darken all your triumphs.

[Exit.

HONORIA
His threats move me as little, as his love,
Yet for thy sake I can be sad.

ALWORTH
And I
But onely mourn for you.

[Enter **COLONEL** with a Pistol, and **TRAVERSE**.

He is return'd,
And with him the first poisoner of our peace;
What horrour next?

COLONEL
Your happiness is now
Within your reach, kill but that fellow, and
Possess her by my gift, the act once done
By my command secures thee.

HONORIA
He shall make
His passage to thee through my heart.

TRAVERSE
I thank you
For your great promise and employment, Sir,
But take your tool agen,

COLONEL
Did you not love her?

TRAVERSE
Yes infinitely, but scorn your Hangmans Office:
I have done too much alreadie; but if Madam,
The memorie of my base surprize have not
Weig'd me down past all fathom of your mercy,
I can ask you forgiveness in my heart,
And suffer all his Tyrannie, to expiate
My black offence to you, and to that Gentleman.

COLONEL
Are you so resolute?

TRAVERSE
Were I assur'd
There were no punishment to attend this murder
Here, nor hereafter, could she pardon this
Bloodie assassination, and Alworth
Forgive me, when his soul is gliding through
The purple stream, and mounting up to fill
Some happie star, would she herself consent
To be the great reward of the black deed,
I should abhor the Patricide.

COLONEL
Is't so? expect my next return.

[Exit **ALWORTH**

Sir, you have shewn a penitence would strike
A marble through, and this return to pietie,
Hath chang'd our anger into Admiration.

HONORIA
Sir, we have now no thoughts, but what are fil'd,
With a desire you call us to your friendship;
Live happie, and adorn by your example
Of justice, the most honoured robe you wear.

[Enter **COLONEL, ALAMODE, FULBANKE, SQUANDERBAG** and **AURELIA MAMMON.**

COLONEL
Nay ye shall witness all my resolution;
Your hand, deer Madam, Alworth take from me
Thy own Honoria, it were impious
To keep you a minute longer in your fears,
Your loves deserve my admiration, not
My anger, and I cheerfully resign
All my ambitions, live you happie both
As I am in this conquest of my self:
I lov'd Honoria well, but justice better.
But Madam, though you must be Alworths Bride,
Yet give me leave to call you Mistress, I
Can be your servant still, and by your influence
Upon me, steer my actions, and keep
My passions in as much obedience,
As any Soldier I command, and Alworth
Be you so just, to tell the world that takes
Delight to snarl, and catch at every errour
In our profession: I am no enemy
To Arts, but can take pleasure to reward
Learning, with all due honour, be your self
The example.

ALWORTH
You are perfect
In all that's noble, and it were a sin
Not to proclaim it.

TRAVERSE
Sir, This act will crown
Your name for ever.

COLONEL
Make your peace with Honoria,
Tis done, and we owe all we can call happy
To your justice, Sir.
[to **AURELIA MAMMON**]
Madam, you look upon us through some cloud,
None should be worn this day, and here are some
Did wear the title of your servant. Fulbank—

FULBANKE
Oh you are trulie noble, I ever honoured my Ladie.

COLONEL
Travers, Alamode,

SQUANDERBAG

Please you to name me in the list, I can
Be as much a servant to this Ladie, as
The best of these.

COLONEL

Stand forth, and plead your merits.

AURELIA MAMMON

I excuse them,
Your pardon Sir, I think the best in all the
File unworthie of me.

COLONEL

Plain truth, Gentlemen.

AURELIA MAMMON

I could give reasons, but I have no humor
To spoil some reputations in publique.

ALAMODE

I told you what a Gypsie 'twas.

AURELIA MAMMON

Some may
Traduce my fame, and charge me with a levity
And frequent change, but I have been less constant,
Because I found no man had wit enough
To manage me, or worth enough to invite
The stay of my affections. I acknowledge
The Citizen doth promise fair, but breaks:
Lawyers are cunning, but I love not snares:
The Courtier has no care of his own body;
The Countrey-man had no wit but in his acres:
And for you, Sir, your name is Squanderbag,
What would you do with Mammon, cannot keep her?
Beside, these men had the bad luck to court me
When I was swaid by an evil genius,
Which now has left me. I see alreadie
A nobler path, and till I finde a man
Knows how to love, and govern me with temperance,
I lay my self an humble servant at
Honoria's feet; your pardon to my past
Neglects, will make me cheerfull to attend you.

COLONEL

Nay, since y'are come to be my fellow-servant,
If you please, Madam, we may approach neerer;

What think you of me, shall I present my self
A servant to your favour?

AURELIA MAMMON
Sir, you are pleasant.

COLONEL
I shall be so, if you accept my service;
Though I am a Soldier, I can love, and do
All duties may become your worth and honour.

AURELIA MAMMON
I blush to say how much I am unworthie,
But I shall meet you honourably.

COLONEL
A match, seal it.

[Salute.

FULBANKE
He has don't it compendiously; But Sir, you know—

COLONEL
Yes, I know very well what you would say,
But this fair Lady's mine, and I'll deserve her:
Wealth has alreadie made you mad, we have been
Out of the Sun a great while, I invite
You all my guests to day, and Ladie Mammons,
Do me that honour.

FULBANKE
There is no remedie.

[Enter **MASLIN** strip'd.

ALAMODE
'Tis well you scap'd with loss of Mammon.

COLONEL
What anti-Masquers this?

AURELIA MAMMON
'Tis Mr. Maslin.

CAPTAIN
This fellow wod not bend, and so they broke him.

MASLIN

You look like the Commander in chief
Of this Militia.

COLONEL

What then?

MASLIN

I have a suit to you.

COLONEL

A suit? methinks y'are naked.

MASLIN

I know not, but on my knees I beg their pardon
That made me so, they plunder'd me so quaintly,
They are the nimblest Hocus Pocus's
That e're threw dice for hemp.

COLONEL

I am glad they fitted you.

MASLIN

No Sir, it was the Tailor fitted me.

COLONEL

So, and they unfitted you.

MASLIN

But with what art, how most compendiously
They made me an Adamite, Sir—

COLONEL

Let's hear your wonder.

MASLIN

One ill look'd fellow did but swear an oath,
And my hat flew up with the very wind of it,
And fell upon a head, that stood bare for it
Full three yards off:
Another did but squint upon my legs,
And my boots vanish'd with the spurs upon'em;
Cloak, doublet, jerkin, all convenient broad cloth,
Three pile of wool, went from me at one motion;
No bars nor buttons could prevail a minute,
They broke into my bodie with that nimble
Burglarie; I was undone e're I could wink:
But when my narrow shirt came o're my shoulders,

I thought't had been my skin, at every twitch
I roar'd, and gave my self gone for a Rabbet
For the next Officers supper.

COLONEL
In good time.

MASLIN
But truth appear'd when I was strip'd, their charitie
Left me my breeches, but the good old gold
Could not have leave to bear 'em companie,
That was defaulk'd miraculously by a Mirmidon
That had lost both his hands—

ALAMODE
Lost both his hands,
How could he take your money?

MASLIN
With his stumps, Sir,
He routed both my pockets with his stumps;
Oh the knack some men have to fetch out money.

COLONEL
He is pleasant, see his wardrobe be restord.

MASLIN
Shall I be warm agen, Oh Madam —

SQUANDERBAG
Be not too sawcie, she is now exalted
Above your sphere.

FULBANKE
Oh Mr. Maslin, we are all undone.

MASLIN
So am I, they have not left me a shirt.

COLONEL
All faults, where we have power this day, are pardon'd.

ALAMODE
Happiness crown your loves!

COLONEL
Now to the Priest,
Whose work is onely wanting to confirm us:

Alworth, lead on your fairest Bride, remember
We are both servants to Honoria.

ALWORTH
To shew I can obey you Sir, come Madam.
The Birth of Heaven, and the Earths Morningstar,

COLONEL
Our life of Peace, and the true soul of
War.

[Exeunt.

JAMES SHIRLEY – A CONCISE BIBLIOGRAPHY

The following includes years of first publication, and of performance if known, together with dates of licensing by the Master of the Revels if available.

Tragedies
The Maid's Revenge (licensed 9 Feb. 1626; printed, 1639)
The Traitor (licensed 4 May 1631; printed, 1635)
Love's Cruelty (licensed 14 Nov. 1631; printed, 1640)
The Politician (acted, 1639; printed, 1655)
The Cardinal (licensed 25 May 1641; printed, 1652).

Tragicomedies
The Grateful Servant (licensed 3 Nov. 1629 as The Faithful Servant; printed 1630)
The Young Admiral (licensed 3 July 1633; printed 1637)
The Coronation (licensed 6 Feb. 1635, as Shirley's, but printed in 1640 as a work of John Fletcher)
The Duke's Mistress (licensed 18 Jan. 1636; printed 1638)
The Gentleman of Venice (licensed 30 Oct. 1639; printed 1655)
The Doubtful Heir (printed 1652), licensed as Rosania, or Love's Victory in 1640
The Imposture (licensed 10 Nov. 1640; printed 1652)
The Court Secret (printed 1653).

Comedies
Love Tricks, or the School of Complement (licensed 10 Feb. 1625; printed under its subtitle, 1631)
The Wedding (ca. 1626; printed 1629)
The Brothers (licensed 4 Nov. 1626; printed 1652)
The Witty Fair One (licensed 3 Oct. 1628; printed 1633)
The Humorous Courtier (licensed 17 May 1631; printed 1640).
The Changes, or Love in a Maze (licensed 10 Jan. 1632; printed 1639)
Hyde Park (licensed 20 April 1632; printed 1637)
The Ball (licensed 16 Nov. 1632; printed 1639)
The Bird in a Cage, or The Beauties (licensed 21 Jan. 1633; printed 1633)
The Gamester (licensed 11 Nov. 1633; printed 1637)

The Example (licensed 24 June 1634; printed 1637)
The Opportunity (licensed 29 Nov. 1634; printed 1640)
The Lady of Pleasure (licensed 15 Oct. 1635; printed 1637)
The Royal Master (acted and printed 1638)
The Constant Maid, or Love Will Find Out the Way (printed 1640)
The Sisters (licensed 26 April 1642; printed 1653).
Honoria and Mammon (printed 1659)

Dramas

A Contention for Honor and Riches (printed 1633), morality play
The Triumph of Peace (licensed 3 Feb. 1634; printed 1634), masque
The Arcadia (printed 1640), pastoral tragicomedy
St. Patrick for Ireland (printed 1640), neo-miracle play
The Triumph of Beauty (ca. 1640; printed 1646), masque
The Contention of Ajax and Ulysses (printed 1659), entertainment
Cupid and Death (performed 26 March 1653; printed 1659), masque

www.ingramcontent.com/pod-product-compliance
Lightning Source LLC
Chambersburg PA
CBHW060133050426
42448CB00010B/2096